Y0-BRD-457

E-Government

E-Government

From Vision to Implementation

A PRACTICAL GUIDE WITH CASE STUDIES

Subhash Bhatnagar

SAGE Publications
New Delhi/Thousand Oaks/London

Copyright © Subhash Bhatnagar, 2004

All rights reserved. No part of this book may be reproduced or utilised in any form or by any means, electronic or mechanical, including photocopying, recording or by any information storage or retrieval system, without permission in writing from the publisher.

First published in 2004 by

Sage Publications India Pvt Ltd
B-42, Panchsheel Enclave
New Delhi 110 017

Sage Publications Inc
2455 Teller Road
Thousand Oaks, California 91320

Sage Publications Ltd
1 Oliver's Yard, 55 City Road
London EC1Y 1SP

Published by Tejeshwar Singh for Sage Publications India Pvt Ltd, typeset in 10 pt CG Times by Star Compugraphics Private Limited, New Delhi and printed at Chaman Enterprises, New Delhi.

Library of Congress Cataloging-in-Publication Data

Bhatnagar, Subhash C.
   E-government: from vision to implementation: a practical guide with case studies/ Subhash Bhatnagar.
      p. cm.
   Includes bibliographical references and index.
   1. Internet in public administration—Developing countries. 2. Internet in public administration—Developing countries—Case studies. I. Title.
   JF1525.A8B43   352.3'8'02854678—dc22   2004   2004011712

ISBN: 0–7619–3259–3 (US–HB)   81–7829–393–5 (India–HB)
          0–7619–3260–7 (US–PB)   81–7829–394–3 (India–PB)

Sage Production Team: Payal Dhar, Vineeta Rai, Sushanta Gayen and Santosh Rawat

Contents

List of Tables

Tables

List of Figures

Figures

List of Boxes

Preface

For the last three decades I have been interested in the application of information and communication technologies (ICTs) for development. India has always been a fertile ground for innovations in ICT applications for rural development. Several successful pilots were developed by entrepreneurs amongst civil servants. I was involved in an action research project in Surendra Nagar district of Gujarat where a mini-computer was installed at the collectorate in 1985. A team of researchers attempted to develop applications that would support planning and monitoring of development programmes at the district level. Fifty district collectors came together in 1985 in a workshop at the Indian Institute of Management (IIM), Ahmedabad, to discuss the Surendra Nagar project and share their own experiences of ICT use in district administration. Some of these pilots were scaled up through central government initiatives, but for many years the overall impact of ICTs on India's development remained marginal.

Interest in ICT use by governments revived in the late 1990s in India and other parts of the developing world. India began to emerge as an important software development centre. Several IT multinationals companies set up offices in India. Internet and e-commerce became buzzwords. India also progressed towards a more liberalised economy. Anecdotes about e-government projects began to trickle in from many developing countries. Andhra Pradesh in India pioneered with a few applications. There was considerable interest in the vendor community as it saw a large market opportunity.

In October 1999 IIM Ahmedabad set up a Centre for Electronic Governance with support from three private sector companies. I was asked to coordinate the activities of the new centre. At the same time I was also coordinating the work of the Telecom Policy Research Centre at the institute. The work of these two centres provided me the opportunity to look at emerging uses of ICT, particularly within the government and the rural sector.

In the year 2000 IIM Ahmedabad organised a workshop on ICT and Rural Development in India in which several project leaders of innovative projects shared their experiences. Some significant e-government projects from Andhra Pradesh were also presented. Publication of the workshop proceedings was well received, encouraging me to undertake further case research on ICT uses within the government. Soon thereafter, I moved to Washington DC on a two-year assignment with the Public Sector Group within the Poverty Reduction and Economic Management Network of the World Bank to mainstream e-government into the lending activities of the World Bank. The assignment provided me the opportunity to broaden my horizon by understanding the developments in the use of ICTs within the government in a number of developing countries. I was able to document two dozen case studies from many developing countries of the world. I was also involved in assessing the e-government plans of many countries and in providing advice to such countries.

This book is a result of the two years of intensive work done at the World Bank in which the field experience had to distilled and communicated to Bank staff through workshops and training programmes.

The book provides practical insights for IT professionals, civil servants and managers from multilateral institutions interested in the implementation of e-government. The book is intended to serve as a practical guide for developing e-government at a local, state or national level. It should be useful for practitioners, researchers as well as students. Twelve case studies have been included, which provide learning for different facets of e-government. Each case study is structured in a standard format to highlight the application context and learning from the experience. The cases are rich enough for readers to draw additional lessons. These cases can be used as a basis of class discussion for key issues in implementing ICT applications. Even though many of the cases are drawn from India and my own experience and understanding of the subject has been moulded by the Indian experience, the issues of implementing e-government are similar across the world. The book includes cases from countries other than India and should be equally useful to professionals, academics and students from any part of the world.

Material for this book has been drawn from a variety of sources, including many conceptual notes and cases that I had developed while working for the Indian Institute of Management (IIM), Ahmedabad, and during the last four years for the World Bank. I am grateful for the support extended to me by both the institutions to carry out case research.

In documenting nine Indian case studies that are carried in this book, I was greatly helped by the civil servants who had implemented these projects. I wish to thank Rajeev Chawla, Nitesh Vyas, J. Sathyanarayana, Arvind Kumar, P. Panneervel, A. Vijaya Lakshmi and R. Padma for facilitating field visits as well as their contribution in drafting the cases.

I wish to acknowledge the contribution of Arsala Deane, staff at the World Bank who helped me with the analysis of some cases and co-authored a note with me. Thanks are also due to Jeffrey Rinne, another colleague at the World Bank who edited several of the cases. Amongst the IIM Ahmedabad staff, I specially wish to thank Animesh Rathore, who helped in research for two case studies included in the book. Thanks are also due to Urmil Anjaria, my secretary, who has typed several bits and pieces of text that went into the book. Final thanks are due to my wife Prof. Deepti Bhatnagar, for encouraging me to undertake this project and providing me with valuable feedback at different stages of the project.

Introduction

E-government applications have emerged rapidly in the developing world. Many countries use e-government as an enabling tool to increase efficiency, enhance transparency, collect more revenue and facilitate public sector reform. While e-government is not a panacea that can improve the performance of the public sector, it is a powerful enabling tool that has aided governments achieve some of their development and administrative reform goals. Although e-government can be a catalyst for change, it is not a complete solution and it must be part of a broader commitment to reform the public sector. Three factors are critical for the successful implementation of e-government. These include willingness to reform, availability of information communications technology (ICT) infrastructure, and the institutional capacity to absorb and manage change.

The book is based on the analysis of two dozen cases from sixteen countries in the developing world where e-government has been implemented to address social and economic development challenges.[1] A number of these case studies have been included in this volume. It should be noted that documented case studies often highlight success stories. There may be a significant number of failed projects amongst the applications that have not been documented. Twelve of these case studies are presented in the book. Countries that are featured in the case studies are considered pioneers in developing innovative e-applications.

In the last ten years ICT investment by governments in developing countries has witnessed a dramatic increase. Most developing countries are using ICT to modernise and increase internal efficiency as well as improve service delivery. As a result, many developing countries have either embarked on e-government or are in the process of creating strategies. The book is intended to provide practical guidelines on selection

---

[1] The main source is the documentation of case studies carried on the web site of Public Sector Group at the World Bank, http://www1.worldbank.org/publicsector/egov. Another source is the IDPM web site of Manchester University, http://www.mceg.org.uk/links.htm. Four detailed cost–benefit evaluations of Indian projects are available at http://www1.worldbank.org/publicsector/bnpp/egovupdate.htm.

of application areas, project design, strategy and implementation. Analysis of existing applications provide useful insights into the emerging trends of e-government in the developing world and also provide lessons on the many ways to overcome challenges in implementation.

The book also documents the benefits and impact of e-government on public sector reform, poverty reduction and empowerment. The book identifies critical success factors that must be present for e-government applications to have an impact on development and improving governance. Critical success factors such as defining project goals that are measurable and focused on governance reform, institutional capacity and presence of reform-minded leadership are discussed in detail. Although no comprehensive framework exists, several countries have incorporated these factors into the design of their e-government programmes in many creative ways.

The book presents the material in seven chapters. Chapter 1 provides a comprehensive definition of e-government. Chapter 2 provides an understanding of e-government, how it has emerged and for what purposes it has been used in developing countries. These have included services to citizens, such as transactions involved in obtaining land deeds, certificates and permits, taxes, and services to businesses such as customs, business licences and procurement. The goals and delivery models used for e-government differ from those of developed countries. Creative approaches have been used to bridge the literacy, infrastructure and digital divides in service delivery. Often a hybrid form of service delivery is used, combining manual and online mechanisms.

Chapter 3 explores the benefits and impact of e-government on good governance, empowerment and poverty reduction. The section details the effects of e-government applications on enhancement of transparency, reduction of corruption, improvement of service delivery and empowerment. Evidence shows that e-government has had a significant impact on broader governance goals where political leadership and a commitment to reform have been present.

Chapter 4 describes best practices in project design and managing change. Particular attention is given to the need for a well-defined project scope, goals and target audience. E-government projects must be accompanied by process re-engineering of back-office procedures. Processes should be re-engineered to reduce discretionary powers of civil servants and make data and decisions more transparent rather than to downsize the department. This is necessary to deliver effective and speedy service delivery with reduced corruption. Many e-government projects invest too little effort in process re-engineering because this exercise meets significant internal resistance from civil servants who fear losing their jobs and their power.

Chapter 5 provides practical guidelines for the creation of a country-level strategy and implementation plan. The guidelines are drawn from best practices that document both risks and merits of different strategies that have been used in developing countries. One lesson of particular importance is the need for departments to have ownership of e-government projects. National strategy and standards are important in the long run for establishing interoperability. However, government departments need to take the lead in design, implementation and developing pilots that bring significant benefits to the target users. Chapter 5 also emphasises the need for the evaluation of e-government projects, and proposes a methodology for evaluation and risk analysis for choosing appropriate pilots. Many projects rely on purely anecdotal evidence to measure success. This has left little comprehensive information about the success factors and ways to tackle failure in e-government. The basic methodology provided in this section draws from four independent evaluations of e-government projects in India.

Chapter 6 looks ahead and also summarises some of the important learnings that emerge from the book. Chapter 7 presents twelve case studies of e-government applications. These cases cover the whole range—serving different types of clients (citizens, business); focusing on different purposes (improving service delivery, transparency, increasing tax revenue, controlling government expenditure, empowering rural communities); and built by different tiers of government (federal, state and local). All the cases are structured in a similar format. They explain the application context, new approaches embodied in the e-government application, challenges faced during implementation, benefits delivered and costs incurred. The final section discusses key lessons that can be drawn from the case study. Reference to these cases has been made in the early chapters that present the analysis of the 'what', 'why' and 'how' of e-government.

The book is written for a diverse audience. It analyses the trends that have emerged in developing countries and how e-government is used to further development and reform goals. The book recognises many different challenges that must be overcome for implementation of e-government and many diverse approaches that can be used to tackle these challenges. Successful e-government will be shaped by local contexts. The book provides a few guidelines that emerge from worldwide experience.

A discussion of e-government can cover several perspectives. A technical perspective will focus on technical architecture of solutions; choice of technology and platforms; different ways of handling security and electronic payments. A public administration perspective may focus on outcomes—impact on efficiency, transparency and corruption. An economic perspective will focus on the questions of investments, cost and benefits. A managerial perspective may focus on systems analysis, re-engineering and management of change. It requires a multi-disciplinary approach to plan and implement e-government. While not emphasising technology, the book attempts to integrate the many different perspectives.

1

E-Government:
Definition and Scope

Governments have been engaged in deploying information and communication technologies (ICTs) for several decades to increase the efficiency and effectiveness of their functioning. Early applications were focused on building management information systems for planning and monitoring. Many large projects have been undertaken and there have been prominent failures.[1] The record of using ICT to gain any benefit has been quite dismal. However, the advent of the Internet and its use in advocacy, distance learning, fostering participation and particularly in delivery of information and services to citizens by some countries has once again revived the hope that ICTs can deliver value commensurate with investments.

Successful use of the Internet by advocacy groups to promote their view point has caught the imagination of some governments.[2] The Internet is seen as a tool for empowerment of disadvantaged groups and rural communities. Some experiments in infusing greater democracy and participation in the functioning of private sector companies through the use of tools of decision conferencing and electronic meeting rooms have prompted new experiments in the use of similar tools in the context of citizen's engagement in the governing process. Widespread access to the Internet has prompted some politicians to put forth ideas about direct democracy.[3]

[1] According to one survey, only 15 per cent of e-government projects are successful, 35 per cent are total failures and 55 per cent partial failures. See Richard Heeks, 'Success and Failure Rates of eGovernment in Developing/Transitional Countries: Overview', Institute for Development Policy and Management, University of Manchester, March 2003, http://www.e-devexchange.org/eGov/sfoverview.htm.

[2] 'Mexican Women's Movement Makes Internet Work for Women', http://www. connected.org/women/erika.html.

[3] Murray N. Rothbard, 'Perot: The Constitution, and Direct Democracy', in *Making Economic Sense*. Auburn, AL: Mises Institute, 1992, pp. 4–5.

For example, the Minnesota Electronic Democracy Project (MN E-D Project) was founded in July 1994 by Steven Clift to study the impact of new communications technologies on government organisations and the political process.[4] Originally, the project was designed to create a place on the Internet for the public to access information from the candidates and about the candidates running for office in the upcoming state and national elections in November 1994. It had many features that collectively made the experiment unique. It was designed for the electoral process; it was locally based; it was organised by citizens and civic organisations; it sought to distribute political information directly from the candidates; and it featured an interactive public forum. Most important was the combination of the contacts created with candidates and the e-mail-based listserve for citizen dialogue being preserved in a hypermail archive at the Twin Cities Freenet. All such experiments within local governments and political parties have come to be collectively known as e-democracy.

Effectiveness of distance learning and experiments with computer-assisted learning in programmes have demonstrated the potential of ICT in promoting literacy and education in remote areas.[5] With the growth of the Internet within the educational system, new opportunities of virtual classrooms/degrees have been demonstrated. Many governments have launched initiatives to connect schools.

After the World Development Report placed knowledge at the core of the development agenda, there has been much focus on the problems of digital divide.[6] Many nations have come to believe that unless they address the problem of digital divide by expanding their Internet infrastructure, they will not be able to participate in the global economy and will further lag behind. Policies for the growth of the Internet and equitable distribution of access are being designed.

For a while, all these uses of ICTs within the government to achieve different objectives and goals and associated policies for promoting the

[4] G. Scott Aikens, 'History of the Minnesota Electronic Democracy Project', http://www.isoc.org/isoc/whatis/conferences/inet/96/proceedings/e9/e9_1.htm.

[5] Like PLATO, which began in 1963 with Control Data and University of Illinois using a grant from the National Science Foundation to develop the technology and content for a computer-assisted instructional system (http://www.plato.com), and World Links, which connects nearly 200,000 students from twenty developing countries with students in developed countries, (http://www.world-links.org/english/).

[6] *World Development Report 1998–99*, http://www.worldbank.org/wdr/wdr98/contents.htm.

use of ICTs were being collectively labelled as e-government in some articles.[7]

The term e-government is of recent origin and there is no commonly accepted definition. Major English dictionaries do not list the word e-government or electronic government. The term was perhaps coined about a decade ago after the success of electronic commerce to represent a public sector equivalent of e-commerce. The term is used in a loose manner to describe the legacy of any kind of use of information and communication technology within the public sector. For those who see it as some form of extension of e-commerce to the domain of the government, it represents the use of the Internet to deliver information and services by the government.

Analogous to the concept of e-commerce, which brings customers closer to businesses (B2C) and enables businesses to transact with each other (B2B) more efficiently, e-government aims to make the interaction between government and citizens (G2C); government and business enterprises (G2B) and inter-agency dealing (G2G) friendly, convenient, transparent and less expensive. E-commerce has evolved through four stages: pure publishing; interactivity; completing transactions and delivery. Similar stages have been defined for assessing the maturity of e-government. In this book we take a broader view. E-government is understood as the use of ICT to promote more efficient and cost-effective government, facilitate more convenient government services, allow greater public access to information, and make government more accountable to citizens.[8]

Traditionally, the interaction between a citizen or business and a government agency took place in a government office. With emerging information and communication technologies it is possible to locate service centres closer to the clients. Such centres may consist of an unattended

---

[7] See Richard Heeks, 'E-government for Development: Basic Definitions Page', Institute for Development Policy and Management, University of Manchester, 2004, http://www.egov4dev.org/egovdefn.htm.

[8] For various definitions and scope of e-government, see World Bank, 'E*Government', http://www1.worldbank.org/publicsector/egov/index.htm and http://www.archives.nysed.gov/pubs/recmgmt/egovernment/definiti.htm; 'Pacific Council on International Policy, Roadmap for E-Government in the Developing World', April 2002, www.pacificcouncil.org; *Economist*, 'Survey: Government and the Internet', 24–30 June 2000. E. Tambouris, S. Gorilas and G. Boukis, 'Investigation of Electronic Government', http://www.egov-project.org/egovsite/tambouris_panhellenic.pdf; J. Caldow, 'The Quest for Electronic Government: A Defining Vision', Company Report, IBM Corporation, http://www.ieg.ibm.com.

kiosk in the government agency, a service kiosk located close to the client or the use of a personal computer in the home or office.

E-government applications normally evolve through a four-stage process as depicted in Figure 1.1.[9] The first stage includes the publication of information on a web site for citizens to seek knowledge about procedures governing the delivery of different services. The second stage allows for interactivity online. Clients can download applications for receiving services. The third stage involves electronic delivery of documents. The fourth stage results in electronic delivery of services where more than one department may be involved in processing a request or service. Models with public–private partnerships are offered.

Figure 1.1
E-Government Evolution: Four Critical Stages

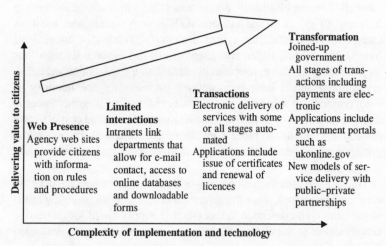

E-government comprises of an alignment of ICT infrastructures, institutional reform, business processes and service content towards provision of high-quality and value-added e-services to citizens and businesses. Omnipresent e-government services require relaxation of time, place and other accessibility constraints, and compliance to architectural principles such as true one-stop services and life-event orientation. Critical issues arise with respect to prioritisation and pilot scoping of e-government services projects, exploitation of multi-device/multi-channel access

---

[9] *Gartner Dataquest*, November 2000.

technologies, re-engineering and security of back-end ICT infrastructure as well as evaluation of operational schemes.

The term e-government is sometimes confused with e-governance and the two terms are often used interchangeably. E-governance has been defined as the process of enabling transactions between concerned groups and the government through multiple channels by linking all transaction points, decision points, enforcing/implementation points and repositories of data using information and communication technologies, to improve the efficiency, transparency, accountability and effectiveness of a government.[10]

Governance is defined as *the manner in which power is exercised in the management of a country's economic and social resources for development*.[11] Implicit in the reference to 'power' is the concept of accountability. E-governance should, therefore, also focus on the *accountability* of public officials and their abuse of power in the management of public resources, as distinguished from *efficiency*, which may be taken as falling under the broader fabric of 'good government'. It can be argued that the efficiency of government, and its impact on the intended beneficiaries of public services, is crucially linked to the presence or absence of public accountability. The heavy focus on the former, to the neglect of the latter, goes far to explain why reforms often fail. This view of e-governance overlaps considerably with the definition of e-government that we have used in the book.

Definitions often miss out on the major distinction between e-governance and e-government. Governance is a broader concept that encompasses the state's institutional arrangements, decision-making processes, implementation capacity and the relationship between government officials and the public. E-governance is the use of ICT by the government, civil society and political institutions to engage citizens through dialogue and feedback to promote their greater participation in the process of governance of these institutions. For example e-governance covers the use of the Internet by politicians and political parties to elicit views from their constituencies in an efficient manner or the ability of civil society to publicise views that are in conflict with the ruling powers. E-governance consist of two distinct but intimately intertwined dimensions: one political

[10] Anil Srivastava, 'E-Governance or Development What Comes First: Issues and Correlations', Syracuse: The Maxwell School of Citizenship and Public Affairs, Syracuse University.

[11] World Bank, *Governance and Development*. Washington, DC: World Bank, 1992, http://publications.worldbank.org/ecommerce/catalog/product?item_id=194297.

and the other technical, relating to issues of efficiency and public management. With some overlapping goals between the two, e-government can be viewed as a subset of e-governance, and its focus is largely on improving administrative efficiency and reducing administrative corruption.

The term e-government as it is used and understood in this book is based on the following definition.

E-government is about a process of reform in the way governments work, shares information and delivers services to external and internal clients. Specifically, e-government harnesses information technologies (such as wide area networks,[12] the Internet and mobile computing) to transform relations with citizens, businesses and other arms of government. These technologies can serve a variety of ends: better delivery of government services to citizens; improved interactions with business and industry; citizen empowerment through access to information, or more efficient government management. The resulting benefits can be less corruption, increased transparency, greater convenience, revenue growth and/or cost reductions.

---

[12] A wide area network (WAN) is a geographically dispersed telecommunications network. The term distinguishes a broader telecommunication structure from a local area network. A WAN may be privately owned or rented, but the term usually connotes the inclusion of public (shared user) networks. An intermediate form of network in terms of geography is a metropolitan area network (MAN) (definition from http://searchnetworking.techtarget.com/sDefinition/0,,sid7_gci214117,00.html).

2

Understanding E-Government in Developing Countries

Assessments made by some consulting companies indicate that e-government is in a nascent stage of implementation in both developed and developing countries.[1] Government departments in many developing countries publish information on web sites as a first step towards e-government. Many of these sites are poorly designed and the departments do not update or monitor the quality of information. Initially the publishing of information online was targeted at attracting foreign investments, but as Internet penetration grew in urban areas, many sites began to focus on delivering information and services to citizens and businesses. A large number of developing countries from Asia and Latin America have implemented transaction-oriented e-government applications on a pilot basis. However, only a few of these pilots have been replicated on a wider scale.

The Table 2.1 enumerates documented case studies of e-government applications from different developing countries. The table lists countries where such applications have been developed and identifies a few benefits that have been realised. These applications represent *the low hanging fruit*; applications that deliver significant benefit and yet are not difficult to implement. This table is used as a basis for further analysis to understand the types of clients that have been served, different delivery models that have been used, and purposes for which e-government applications have been built. This chapter also presents salient features of design and implementation, and provides some idea of costs of different projects. Finally some key overall trends are enumerated.

---

[1] United Nations, 'Benchmarking E-government: A Global Perspective—Assessing UN Member States', Division of Public Economics and Public Administration, 2001, http://unpan1.un.org/intradoc/groups/public/documents/un/unpan003984.pdf.

Table 2.1
Some Examples of Successful Projects from Different Countries

Application	Examples	Benefits
Delivering citizen services		
Payment of property taxes, Issue of land titles	CARD in Andhra Pradesh at 230 locations; Bhoomi in rural areas in Karnataka and Maharashtra at 189 locations	Transparency; faster processing for citizens; reduced corruption, increased productivity for offices
Income tax online	Brazil; Jordan; Chile; Mexico	Convenient; quicker refunds; better compliance; cost reduction
Issue of driving licence, motor registration, passport, birth certificate, social security and collection of fines	Citizen service centres (mobile and in shopping malls), Bahia, Brazil; Andhra Pradesh, Karnataka, Gujarat in India; Jordan	Cut delays; several services under one roof; reduced corruption; reduction of intermediaries
Online issue/payment of electricity, telephone and water bills, and fines	E-Seva in Hyderabad; FRIENDS in Kerala	Convenient locations; quicker processing time; customer does many tasks in one visit
Delivery of services to business and industry		
E-procurement	Mexico; Philippines; Brazil; Bulgaria; Chile	Reduce advertisement costs; lower costs due to better prices; transparency
New business registration	Jordan; Jamaica; China	Reduced time and number of visits; convenience in filing tax returns/quicker refunds
Tax collection (sales tax, VAT and corporate income tax)	Gujarat checkpost in India; Cameroon; Chile; Mauritius	Reduced time and number of visits; convenience on filing tax returns/quicker refunds; increase in revenue collection for government
Customs online	A total of 70 countries including India, Philippines, Mauritius and Jamaica	Quicker clearance; less corruption

(Table 2.1 contd.)

Application	Examples	Benefits
Trade facilitation	Dubai; Mauritius; Tunisia; Yemen	Quick turnaround of ships in ports
Municipal services	OPEN, Seoul municipalities; Latin America	Quick permissions and issue of licences, access and permissions
Increased efficiency within government		
Use of e-mail and video conferencing	Government offices in a large number of countries	Usage is low; faster communication; less travel
Document management and work flow for paperless operations	SmartGov in Andhra Pradesh	Speed of processing; traceability of actions; greater accountability
Integrated Financial Management Systems	Computerised treasuries in Karnataka in India; Kosovo; Afghanistan	Better control of expenditure and prevention of frauds
Empowering citizens through access to information		
Publishing budgets central and municipal level	Argentina; India; Turkey	Greater transparency
Publishing project-wise expenditure, name of executing agency of development projects	Panchayat web sites in Karnataka	Transparency and lower corruption
Publishing tips for improving vocational skills in a format understood by all	Pilots in Gyandoot in Madhya Pradesh; Swaminathan Foundation in Pondichery; Kothamale in Sri Lanka	Knowledge of market prices

2.1 Classifying Applications According to the Clients Served

The list of applications above can be divided into four broad categories: delivering citizen services, delivery of services to business and industry, increased efficiency within the government, and empowering citizens through access to information. Potential benefits that could result from applications in these categories are discussed.

Delivering Services to Citizens

The largest number of applications have been built for service delivery to citizens. A number of states in India and countries in Latin America have implemented online delivery systems for municipal licences, transport permits, property registration and tax collection. Departments with regulatory functions have been quick to embrace e-government, while developmental departments such as education and health have been slow. One of the reasons may be that the informational content for regulatory services is making them more amenable to electronic delivery.

Citizens have benefited from reduced delays, availability of many services under one roof, avoiding frequent visits to government departments and reduced corruption. By publishing information (rules and procedures) online, transparency has been increased.

Delivery of Services to Business and Industry

Tax collection, customs and e-procurement have been popular and quickly embraced because they create more efficient means to collect revenue—this being critical for governments that are cash constrained and cannot enforce payment. Investments in such systems tend to have a quicker payback because of increased revenue collection. Businesses also are quick to use these services because they are provided with an easier, hassle-free channel to interact with the government.

Businesses are often burdened with significant administrative roadblocks when interacting with the government. Electronic delivery can reduce the turnaround of licence applications from several weeks to a few days. Rules can be made transparent and consistent across departments. The elimination of intermediaries can reduce the need for bribes, freeing up resources that can be used to increase competitiveness. A number of countries have implemented online business registration, filing of corporate tax and clearance of traded goods through customs, which have in turn reduced the time and costs for businesses and the government in processing taxes, and have lessened corruption.

Increased Efficiency within the Government

E-government can lead to higher productivity. Governments can reduce the number of employees or redeploy them in more productive tasks.

Often the data captured by the electronic system enables tighter monitoring of productivity of employees, easy identification of pressure points for delay and corruption, and accumulation of historical data that can be easily mined for policy analysis. Data can easily be shared across agencies and departments in an electronic form. Costs rarely decrease in the medium term, as multiple channels of service delivery need to be operated. It takes time for citizens to move from traditional departmental channels to electronic channels.

Significant reduction in costs (of paper, storage space and processing time) can result from a paperless environment in which electronic documents flow across workstations for approval and action. There are one-time costs of hardware/software and other operating expenses associated with such applications. Reduction in the administrative burden of decision makers is a very significant benefit as it releases time for important issues of policy and decision making. Applications that focus entirely on internal efficiency are limited, primarily because these are difficult to implement as they encounter resistance from a well-entrenched civil service. Applications for service delivery to citizens and businesses can also improve internal efficiency.

Empowering Citizens through Access to Information

Some countries have used e-government applications to reach out to communities that do not have easy access to government information. Many of these applications, done as pilots, require that government departments invest a significant amount of time in developing content that is relevant and useful to community needs. In rural South Asia and Latin America, a number of these applications have resulted in limited empowerment of communities that previously could not acquire information such as government rules or prices of agricultural commodities either due to physical distance or corruption. A number of governments in Asia, Latin America, and Central and Eastern Europe are using the Internet to increase external accountability through publication of budgets, civil servant assets, and notices of procurement awards and procedures. Providing this kind of information online has increased transparency of government spending and operations, and also enabled civil society to better monitor government performance and activities.

2.2 Practices in Design and Implementation

Developing countries have the advantage of not having a large number of legacy systems. In principle they could leapfrog to an advanced multi-layered architecture in the design of their systems to ensure security, scalability and data sharing across applications. In practice, the lack of resources and technical capacity has produced a great deal of variability in the technical sophistication of e-government applications built in developing countries. Nowhere is it more pronounced than in the large number of web sites put up by various departments. Resource constraints often force departments to use in-house software developers who are not up-to-date in their technical skills and tend to economise on hardware/software purchase.

Many developing countries have adopted a creative approach in designing e-government applications to overcome the digital divide and lack of resources. As a result, e-government applications are quite different from similar applications in industrialised countries where the delivery model is based on self-service through the Internet. Often the design is built around assisted delivery at community service centres, and the process of delivery is a hybrid of automated and manual processes. For example, payment processes in most developing countries are not electronic (Chile and Brazil being exceptions). Payments are still handled by traditional means of cash, check and credit cards. In fact, in many developing countries in Africa and South Asia, credit cards are not used by a majority of citizens. Government service counters are not connected to credit card processing bureaus so that verification cannot be done online. Most countries have, therefore, not implemented an electronic payment gateway. For certain specific applications, such as toll fee, stored value cards are being tried. New technologies such as radio frequency identification have already found a few uses such as collecting toll fee from cars.[2] Many more applications are likely to be found in the coming years.

In the absence of country-wide policies on data standardisation and data sharing, security provisions have not been adequately handled in designing systems. Surprisingly, privacy has not been a major issue for citizens in the developing world. Governments are now recognising the need for authenticating users (particularly in highly distributed environments). Security over networks is becoming an issue and the need for a certification authority is being felt.

[2] For an overview of applications, see Cathy Booth-Thomas, 'The See-It-All Chip', *Time Magazine*, 20 October 2003, pp. 12–17.

The task of integration across departments has been particularly difficult. As a result, applications that involve a few departments and deliver a specific service to a limited constituency have had the most impact. Consequently, local governments have shown the maximum potential.

In countries that use languages other than English, some have been more successful than others in developing a local language interface for their applications. For example, the Middle Eastern countries that use Arabic have been very successful in developing a standard for the local language interface. Similarly in Latin America the use of Spanish is well developed.

2.3 Different Delivery Models for Electronic Services

Many countries that are moving from manual processes to online systems begin with providing online delivery at departmental counters. These services are subsequently moved to conveniently located multi-service centres and/or through an Internet portal.

The first step consists of departments providing services and information online. Citizens interact with a public or private operator who accesses data and information from online terminals located in the premises of the department. If back-end processes are re-engineered, citizens can experience significant benefits in terms of time, costs and number of trips made. This model tends to result in greater departmental ownership—facilitating easier acceptance of change.

The next step, which is becoming popular in countries with limited Internet penetration, is the use of conveniently located service centres in public places. Counters at these service centres are manned by public/private agencies. Multiple services are offered at each location. Such centres can quickly wean away traffic from departmental counters. Building these centres requires coordination between different departments. Services from municipal, state and federal governments can be offered under one roof. The number of such centres are limited as many countries have found that the coordination between departments is difficult. Some countries have outsourced the running of these centres to private operators who add other value-added services such as payment of insurance to augment their income.

Citizen self-service through portals are popular in countries where Internet penetration and skills are high. In Latin America several governments are using this model particularly in the provision of online tax services to businesses and citizens. The portals offer a variety of services and require a completely computerised back-end in various departments. This model requires investment in security and building of mutual trust. Many countries have experienced a gradual build up of usage.[3] Adoption rate has to be driven through training and awareness raising. Building a portal requires strong centralised leadership to facilitate and encourage inter-departmental coordination. Even through inter-departmental portals, self-service is often difficult to achieve, particularly when the service requires approvals from many different departments.

2.4 How Much Does it Cost?

Costs of e-government projects depend on the initial conditions—whether the application is built from scratch replacing an existing manual system or is an extension of an existing computerised system. Major cost elements are hardware and software at the back end, data conversion, training, maintenance and communications infrastructure to link the public access points to the back end. Costs vary quite dramatically according to scope and scale of application. Projects involving web publishing may cost in thousands of dollars (20 to 200), whereas online service delivery portals for a country take millions of dollars to build. Table 2.2 indicates that the cost of a typical project may vary from $50,000 to $56 million.

Given the low rates of Internet penetration, developing countries have to invest heavily in creating the infrastructure for citizen access. The cost of building e-government applications also depends on whether the software is developed or an existing packaged solution is used. Unless inexpensive software developers are available, as in India and China, it is often more costly to make the software than to buy it. Consultant services for re-engineering and change management[4] can also be expensive if they have to be sourced from large multinational firms, which is often

---

[3] For example, in Canada currently only 11 per cent of citizens use the portal even though 60 per cent of citizens have access to Internet.

[4] Change management can be viewed from two perspectives—from those implementing the change and from the recipients of change. Basically it is the processes and steps that an organisation undertakes to manage change. There are two dimensions of change management that must be incorporated into any strategy: the top-down managers' perspective and the bottom-up employees' perspective (definition from http://www.prosci.com/reengineering.htm).

Table 2.2
E-Government Project Investment

Country	Project	Total cost ($)
Brazil	Citizen service centres, poupatempos	1.8 million
India (Andhra Pradesh)	AP CARD online services	4.3 million
India (Andhra Pradesh)	*Mandals* online	13 million
India (Andhra Pradesh)	Voice online delivery of services	400,000
India (Gujarat)	Computerised interstate checkposts	4 million
India (Karnataka)	Bhoomi online land title registration	3.7 million
India (Maharashtra)	Warana village information kiosks	500,000
India (Madhya Pradesh)	Gyandoot community-owned internet kiosks	50,000
Jamaica	Customs online	5.5 million (partial estimate)
Philippines	Customs modernisation	27 million
Philippines	E-procurement pilot project	400,000
Sri Lanka	Online radio pilot project	35,000
Thailand	Tax system	55.8 million
Vietnam	Online services for businesses	200,000

the case as such capabilities do not exist in developing countries. Capacity both to build and manage software are key considerations. Mistakes made in software design can lead to high expenses for correcting them in the future. A balance between software alternatives—open source and proprietary platforms and applications—can provide avenues for reducing costs.

2.5 Goals of E-Government in Developing Countries

A major goal of e-government projects in developed economies is to enhance productivity of both the public and private sector through the leveraging of ICT. E-government has captured the interest of developing countries. There has been a considerable demonstration effect of the constructive difference that e-government has made in advanced economies in the delivery of services, provision of information and internal administration of the public sector. Many developing countries that have developed significant capacity in building IT applications feel that they can leapfrog to take advantage of the new electronic channels that are available for delivering government services. The reasons for investing in e-government are quite diverse. A country's ICT infrastructure and its openness to public sector reform play an important role in determining the types of applications and kinds of goals for which e-government is implemented.

Countries that have an advanced ICT infrastructure invest in e-government because they are faced with a population that expects government to provide services at the same rate of efficiency and speed that is offered by the private sector.

Citizens in developing countries are experiencing a significant improvement in service levels in e-commerce, vis-à-vis the private sector. They feel that if the private sector can make systematic improvements in service delivery, why can the government not use the same technologies? Thus, citizens in some countries are, in fact, asking the government to go online.

Yet other countries are focusing on improving the efficiency of the public sector to increase economic competitiveness. A number of countries have invested in e-government applications that aim to reduce administrative burdens on the private sector and increase foreign direct investment. Governments are also using e-government applications to encourage citizens to move towards self-service to save costs and time for both citizens and the government.

Countries where external accountability institutions are being strengthened often use e-government tools to augment basic democratic principles such as citizen participation, fundamentally altering the contours of democracy and how citizens interact with the government. These governments are involving their citizens in deciding the kind of services they should be offering and the platforms through which these can be delivered.

Other countries, after experiencing early successes, wish to be pioneers in the e-government field. These successes are a source of pride. For example, Brazil launched an electronic voting system. They are very proud that it is a better system than that of the United States. There is a competition taking place amongst developing countries, and also with developed countries, which spurs the development of new applications.

In the last decade many countries have gone through a process of political and economic liberalisation and economic growth under advice from multilateral lending agencies. Many large countries like India and China have grown at 6 to 10 per cent over the last decade. Having completed the first phase of economic policy reform, such countries are now under compulsion to move to the next phase of reform in the field of governance. Governance reform agendas have included e-government pilots that aim to reduce corruption, increase transparency and quality of service. When e-government has been used towards a specific governance goal that is backed by political leadership, it is seen as an effective tool for governance reform by these countries.

Increasingly, governments in the developing world seek to tie e-government with their overall economic and social development goals. For example, in India alleviation of poverty is an important goal and therefore many applications that deliver services online in rural areas are being tried out in spite of numerous infrastructure constraints. These applications have an effect on empowerment, poverty reduction and improving government responsiveness to poor communities who have had little prior access to public services. Bhoomi (Case 7.1) in Karnataka state in India is a striking example where land titles are delivered online to millions of farmers in 15 minutes instead of the earlier practice where bribes had to be paid and it took weeks to obtain a land title. In other cases knowledge relevant to economic activities is being delivered to communities in local languages through rural Internet kiosks.

In Latin America corruption has been a key public issue and, therefore, e-procurement and transparency in public spending have been emphasised. A number of e-government projects in other countries have also focused on reduction of administrative corruption and increase in transparency. E-government can have a direct impact on: (a) reducing the number of intermediaries that citizens need to interact with in order to get a government service; (b) improving government ability to monitor; and (c) disclosing information about government processes and public budget spending to citizens. Increasingly, governments would like to use e-government as a tool to enhance transparency and reduce corruption, although this goal is sometimes not stated publicly as it may create resistance within the civil service.

A country's willingness to adopt basic public sector reform must determine the breadth and scope of e-government applications. Many times e-government applications are used as a catalyst and enabler to further reform. E-government projects are funded with the expectation that these applications will increase efficiency, and bring about more transparency and accountability to citizens. Success in reforms is directly linked to the openness of a government and its interest in pursuing basic reform goals. For example, many e-government applications would be incompatible with a regime that does not promote increased access to information. Several e-government projects have failed because they were not aligned with realistic expectations and the willingness of governments to introduce basic reform. It is critical that e-government projects become more closely aligned with the political context of a country and its pace of reform. A reform agenda needs to be encouraged more broadly and e-government cannot be perceived as a panacea nor the driver of reform.

There is a real danger that some governments may wish to appear to be modernising and may implement e-government without making any serious attempt to reform government functioning. Box 2.1 summarises some key trends in the development of e-government in developing countries that emerge from the discussion in this chapter.

<u>Box 2.1</u>
Key Trends of E-Government in Developing Countries

1. There are widely divergent approaches and goals.One that has demonstrated success in one country is not necessarily replicable in another country.
2. The largest number of applications have been built for service delivery to citizens. Tax collection, customs and e-procurement have been popular and quickly embraced because they create more efficient means to collect revenue—this is critical for governments that are cash constrained and cannot enforce payment. Departments with regulatory functions have been quick to embrace e-government, while developmental departments such as education and health have been slow.
3. There is a large urban/rural ICT divide that forces governments to adopt creative approaches to delivering services over ICT channels to communities with uneven access to ICT networks. Community centres with operator-assisted online counters have been the most popular mode of delivering services.
4. Technical sophistication in design varies a great deal. Sharing of data, scalability of key operations and security have not been adequately reflected in design. So far privacy has not been a major issue for citizens in the developing world.
5. The task of integration across departments has been particularly difficult. As a result, applications that involve a few departments

and deliver a specific service to a limited constituency have had the most impact.

6. There is significant intra-governmental competition between departments that are eager to move forward in implementing e-government.

7. A large number of government departments across all countries have their web sites. However, publishing information online has not had the kind of impact it was expected to create. In most countries citizens are not ready to engage in a dialogue on how they should be governed. Intermediaries (NGOs, grassroot organisations, media) are often required to generate a debate on public issues to draw in citizens.

3

Potential Benefits and Impact of E-Government

E-government has been used by a number of public agencies as an enabling tool that can help achieve broader good governance goals. Some governments are beginning to link their public sector reform initiatives that pursue both social and economic goals with e-government strategies. E-government cannot be considered a magic bullet that can solve governance problems. Accompanied by the right mix of complementary good governance initiatives and tailored to specific institutional contexts, e-government applications have demonstrated meaningful impact on governance and public sector reform goals in many ways, as Table 3.1 shows.

Table 3.1
How can E-Government Impact Good Governance?

Good governance goals	How e-government can help
Increasing Transparency	• Dissemination of government rules and procedures; citizen's charters; government performance data to wider audience • Disclosure of public assets, government budget; procurement information • Making decisions of civil servants available to public
Reducing administrative corruption	• Putting procedures online so that transactions can be easily monitored • Reducing the gatekeeper role of civil servants through automated procedures that limit discretionary powers • Eliminating the need for intermediaries

(Table 3.1 contd.)

(Table 3.1 contd.)

Good governance goals	How e-government can help?
Improving service delivery	• Less time in completing transactions • Reduction of costs associated with travel for citizens to interact with government • Improving government's ability to deliver service to larger segment of population
Improving civil service performance	• Increased ability of managers to monitor task completion rates of civil servants • Improved efficiency of civil servants by automating tedious work • Increased speed and efficiency of inter- and intra-agency workflow and data exchange • Eliminating redundancy of staff
Empowerment	• Providing communities with limited or no access to government with a new channel to receive government services and information • Reducing the brokerage power of intermediaries
Improving government finances	• Reducing cost of transactions for government processes • Increasing revenue by improving audit functions to better track defaulters and plug leakages by reducing corruption • Providing better control of expenditure

This chapter discusses the impact of e-government on good governance. It highlights examples where e-government has delivered concrete benefits by increasing transparency, reducing corruption, improving service delivery, empowering people and enhancing economic goals of good governance. The necessary conditions that can enhance the realisation of benefits are discussed.

3.1 Increased Transparency and Reduced Corruption

Administrative corruption, bribery and extortion not only undermine the efficiency and effectiveness of government, but also open the government to capture by criminal elements linked to public officials and politicians, and consequently demoralise the public service. This puts at risk the whole fabric of society, which in the worst cases may lead to the collapse of the state.

Through its pioneering surveys in recent years, Transparency International (TI) has tried to gauge the extent of corruption in different countries, identify government departments where corruption appears to be most rampant, and establish some reasons why it seems to grow.[1] Two major factors that contribute to the growth of corruption are the low probability of discovery and perceived immunity against prosecution. Secrecy in government, restrictions on access to information by citizens and the media, ill-defined/complex and excessive rules, procedures and regulations can all lead to a low chance of discovery. A lack of transparency in the functioning of government agencies can make it easy for perpetrators to cover their tracks, and unearthing corruption becomes very difficult. The weak character of institutions that are supposed to investigate charges of corruption and prosecute the guilty as well as an inefficient or corrupt judiciary further exacerbate the problem of corruption and facilitate immunity against prosecution. The consequences of administrative corruption are quite severe for developing societies as:

- The largest cost of corruption is borne by the poor.
- Corruption raises cost of doing business for small and medium enterprises by 20 per cent.
- Corruption is an irritant to investors and impedes foreign direct investment flows.
- There is significant loss of revenue to the government.
- Corruption creates a disincentive for honest and efficient employees and citizens.
- Frequent payment of bribes by citizens increases tolerance for corruption; consequently, society begins to value wrong attributes.
- Petty corruption can be organised to collect illicit funds for politicians.
- Petty corruption opportunities lead to bigger corruption in appointments and transfers.

A few applications have demonstrated that e-government can serve as one of the key tools to fight against corruption by opening up government processes and enabling greater public access to information.[2] E-government systems can lead to greater transparency, resulting in

---

[1] Corruption in India: An Empirical Study, *TI India* (news bulletin), January 2003, http://www.ti-bangladesh.org/ti-india/news/.

[2] Subhash Bhatnagar, *E-Government and Access to Information: Global Corruption Report*. London: Profile Books, pp. 24–32.

reduced administrative corruption.[3] If the right procedures are in place, e-government can make financial or administrative transactions traceable and open to challenge by citizenry. Those responsible for particular decisions or activities can be readily identified. By providing enhanced accounting, monitoring and auditing systems, e-government applications can ensure that public finances are fully open to senior managerial and external scrutiny. As the possibility of exposure of wrongdoing is enhanced, the fear of consequent embarrassment can be a deterrent to corrupt practices.

Several case studies of e-government applications from developing countries report some impact on reducing corruption.[4] Amongst the cases included in this book, Bhoomi (Case 7.1) demonstrates a significant impact on corruption whereas, the case of computerised interstate checkposts in Gujarat (Case 7.9) shows that corruption continued unabated one year after implementation. The case on the OPEN project in Korea (7.11) has been widely recognised for its impact on corruption. The case on the CVC web site (7.12) describes a brave attempt to strengthen the institutions that are supposed to check corruption and stigmatise senior civil servants who were being investigated for corrupt practices. Many governments have chosen to go online in departments such as customs, income tax, sales tax and property tax, which have a large interface with citizens or businesses and are perceived to be more corrupt. Procurement by government is also seen to be an area where corruption thrives.

The very process of building an online delivery system requires that rules and procedures be standardised across regions and made explicit (amenable for computer coding). This reduces the discretion and opportunity for arbitrary action available to civil servants in dealing with every applicant on a case-by-case basis. E-government can be used as an entry point for simplification of rules and re-engineering processes.

E-government can lead to centralisation of data, which can be used for improving audit and analysis. Unbiased sampling procedures can be applied for audit purposes. Integration of data across applications can provide improved intelligence. Not all e-government applications have

---

[3] Administrative corruption refers to the intentional distortion of prescribed implementation of existing laws, procedures and regulations to provide an unfair advantage to an individual or a firm in return for an illicit private gain to a public official. For a more detailed discussion, see *Anticorruption in Transition: A Contribution to the Policy Debate*. Washington DC: World Bank 2000.

[4] For example, the cases on Beijing's business e-park, Philippine custom reform and the OPEN system in Seoul municipality report less corruption as one of the benefits: http://www1.worldbank.org/publicsector/egov.

profited from such integration, as the technical challenges in integrating data are considerable (see the case of customs computerisation in India, Case 7.8).

By providing an alternate to a departmental channel for service delivery, e-government introduces competition that improves service levels and lowers corruption. Publishing of government information on the web builds accountability by providing documentation to citizens to substantiate their complaints against corrupt practices.

However, benefits from e-government, such as reduction of corruption opportunities, are often incidental and not part of the design objectives. To extract maximum benefit from such applications, some features that can lead to greater transparency and accountability need to be consciously built in the design objectives.[5]

There is an implicit hierarchy and sequentiality of objectives on which e-government applications must focus to reduce corruption. Increasing access to information, presenting the information in a manner that leads to transparency of rules and their application in specific decisions, and increasing accountability by building the ability to trace decisions/actions to individual civil servants represent the successive stages in the hierarchy.

All these objectives in tandem can curb corruption significantly, and ignoring some of them can defeat the whole purpose. For example, numerous web sites created by government departments are ineffective because they tend to focus on the single objective of providing electronic access to information.[6] Not enough effort is made to ensure that transparency and accountability are increased.

Table 3.2 presents the type of information where greater transparency can be enabled through e-government applications, which in turn can

[5] Gopakumar Krishnan, 'Increasing Information Access to Improve Political Accountability & Participation', Third Annual Conference of the ABD/OECD Anti-Corruption Initiative for Asia Pacific, Tokyo, 28–30 November 2001.

[6] See Katherine Reilly, 'An External Evaluation of Central American Ministry of Environment Websites: Exploring Methodology, Policy Advocacy and E-Democracy', Working Paper #2, August 2001, http://katherine.reilly.net/e-governance/reports.html, who quotes a 1998 OECD study that reported: 'Many home pages have been mounted less for reasons of information and education than for reasons of prestige—to show that the government or department in question is "*WITH IT*" and not lagging behind others in the new digital world'.

A September 2001 article in the Costa Rican newspaper *El Financiero* stated that, while some innovative online government services are emerging, most Central American government web sites are brochures with static information.

create disincentives for corrupt officials and businesses by increasing the chances of exposure.

Table 3.2
Transparency through E-Government Applications

Type of information being made transparent	Resulting benefits	Illustrations of e-government applications
Rules and procedures governing services; public officials responsible for different tasks; citizen's charter; enhancing citizen's exposure	Leads to standardised procedures for delivery of service; citizens can resist attempts to delay processing; reduces arbitrariness, e.g., demand for additional documents	Web sites of government departments in many countries
Information about decisions and actions of government functionaries, including outcome and process, e.g., award of contracts and licence, allocation of resources	Exposure of corruption and improved accountability	E-procurement in Chile, Philippines (Case 7.7)
Data about individual entities in government records, e.g., as land records, comments on application for licence, bill of entry for goods, status of tax payments	Exposure of manipulation for exchange of bribe and corruption	Bhoomi, online land records in Karnataka (Case 7.1); OPEN in Seoul, Korea (7.11)
Information on performance of economy, e.g., statistical employment, income, trade etc.; performance indicator for government departments	Civic engagement in governance; greater accountability	CRISTAL budget disclosure in Argentina (see Box 3.2)
Names of citizens with large outstanding loans, taxes; civil servants under investigation or convicted; index of corruption; performance of investigating agencies	A kind of punishment for the corrupt through public exposure	CVC web site, India (see Box 3.2)
Disclosure of assets, income; profile of election candidates, elected representatives, ministers and civil servants	Creates disincentive for corruption by creating fear of exposure	Open secrets in the US (7.12); Public Affairs Council, India[7]

[7] See a report by Public Affairs Centre, 'State of the Art as Art of the State: Public Feedback on Egovernance', Bangalore, June 2000, http://www.pacindia.org/.

As indicated in Table 3.2, publication of budgetary allocations and expenditure on the web, systems for tracking status of applications for a variety of licences, sharing citizen's charter and performance data on the web are all known to increase accountability. However, increasing availability of information on the Internet does not mean that citizens will automatically use the information to demand greater accountability. The proportion willing to be constantly engaged in the process of governance is very small. Conscious efforts are required to drive citizens to the portal through advertising campaigns and education. Intermediaries that can analyse such information and highlight exceptional conditions that deserve citizens' attention are needed (see Box 3.1).

<u>Box 3.1</u>
Center for Responsive Politics, USA

The center's web site, interestingly called 'an opensecrets guide' illustrates the constructive role of intermediaries in presenting information to citizens in a format that makes it actionable and allows citizens to make a comparative judgment on the openness of campaign finances of different Congresspeople. The analysis is based on data that is in the public domain, but not in a form that illuminates any corrupt practice. In a recent example, the site provided timely analysis of voting patterns in the House of Representatives on a Bill that pitted long-distance telecom companies against the baby bells. The analysis correlated the voting pattern to the campaign contributions from the two sides and demonstrated that the voting was across party lines, strongly influenced by the size of the contribution.

Traditional media can also play this role. As an alert watchdog, the media needs to highlight such information and generate widespread debate around significant issues of public concern. The web is a new medium for traditional media reporters, and they need to be made aware of the detailed information made available on it through workshops and seminars.

Dealing with Corruption through E-Government: The Way Forward

Much of the evidence linking e-government with reduction in corruption is anecdotal. Only in a couple of cases has the impact on corruption of e-government applications been audited independently. Systematic surveys of citizens and other stakeholders can help establish the linkage more clearly, and will also provide invaluable feedback on the parts of the system that need improvements. There is some evidence that use of ICT in government can also enhance opportunities for corruption.[8]

E-government can be used to combat corruption in two ways. First, it can become one of the key components of a broader anti-corruption strategy as is demonstrated by the OPEN system installed in the Seoul municipality in South Korea (see Case 7.11). Second, service delivery improvement initiatives can be implemented in corrupt departments, specifically targeting transparency and reduced corruption as objectives (as in several cases included in Chapter 7).

By reducing administrative corruption in service delivery, e-government can reduce the tolerance for corruption amongst citizens who would no longer be required to compromise their honesty by paying a bribe to public officials. In addition, a massive societal education effort is required to reinforce fundamental values like honesty.

E-government can lead to transparency provided the legal framework supports free access to information. Until a few years ago most countries still had strict national secrecy laws. These have been repealed in favour of freedom of information laws in the US and much of Europe, but only after decades of lawsuits. Secrecy laws are still in effect in many developing countries. While increasing citizen's access to information, governments must also address risks to privacy and security. Public financial accountability lies at the core of honest government.

It is noteworthy that few, if any, developing countries have in place robust systems to ensure that the spending of public funds is properly accounted for. Budgeting systems are often far from transparent, public accounts often are seriously delayed and highly flawed. Public audits tend to be even more delayed and responsible managers routinely ignore reported deficiencies. Parliamentary scrutiny is often cursory or non-existent. Those responsible for the missing or misused funds are rarely sanctioned except where the actions are politically motivated, and in those cases officials may be unfairly victimised. In these circumstances, transparency can become a powerful tool to foster reform. A few countries (Argentina; see Box 3.2) have posted their official budgets, accounts and audits on a web site, thus enabling them to be scrutinised by citizen

---

[8] Richard Heeks, 'Information Technology and Public Sector Corruption', September 1998, http://idpm.man.ac.uk/idpm/ispsm4.pdf.

Box 3.2
The CRISTAL Web Site, Argentina

The CRISTAL government web site (http://www.cristal.gov.ar) was launched in early 2000 to fulfil the mandate of the September 1999 Fiscal Responsibility Law, which required that the Argentine state make available to its citizens information related to the administration of public funds. The web site discloses and disseminates the information on the use of public funds in Argentina in an easily understandable format, enabling citizens to exercise a more effective control over their political representatives. The information is on the execution of budgets to the lowest level of disaggregation; purchase orders and public contracts; payment orders submitted to the National Treasury; financial and employment data on permanent and contracted staff and those working for projects financed by multilateral organisations; an account of the public debt; inventory of plant and equipment and financial investments; outstanding tax and customs obligations of Argentine companies and individuals; and regulations governing the provision of public services.

Though there were initial problems stemming from lack of information on much of the site, a new version of CRISTAL was launched in August 2000. Between the launch and March 2001, visits to the web site increased by about 200 per cent. The site is currently organised into three thematic areas: 'The State within Reach of All', which explains how public monies are redistributed between the national government and provinces; 'Goals and Results', which gathers information on all national policies to evaluate their management and the manner in which public funds are allocated; and 'Accountability and Representatives', which gathers information related to the fight against corruption, both in government and in the non-government sector. Tutorials explain each of the themes in a lucid fashion. Users can also interact with web site staff and feedback is provided within 24 hours.

For further transparency, CRISTAL itself is externally audited by Foro Transparencia, a coalition made up of fifteen non-government organisations concerned with government transparency. This initiative is proving significant as it seeks to improve governmental transparency, and many agencies have actually started to improve their data gathering practices in response to CRISTAL's requests.

Source: CRISTAL: A Tool for Transparent Government in Argentina, http://www1. worldbank.org/publicsector/egov/cristal_cs.htm.

watch groups, specialised investigative reporters and public policy researchers. By and large, these initiatives are still at a very early stage. However, the potential for promoting greater public financial account-ability in this way is considerable.

E-government reduces corruption by making rules simple and more transparent. Citizens and businesses feel emboldened to question unreasonable rules and procedures, and their arbitrary applications.[9] Although few governments have explicitly stated transparency as a goal, some transparency gains have been achieved through e-applications. Experience from these countries has shown that the objective of trans-parency can be enhanced through the following means:

1. Publishing on the web (Case 7.12 on the CVC web site): A citizens charter stating clearly the service level that a citizen can expect in transacting with the Government; actual perfor-mance in the past on the parameters that measure service levels; details of how governments spend money.
2. A mechanism to receive feedback from citizens on the quality of service offered (see Box 3.3).

<u>Box 3.3</u>
Online Grievance Redressal, Mumbai Municipal Corporation

The system developed by the Greater Mumbai Municipal Corpor-ation (BMC) and the NGO Praja (http://www.praja.org/) allows users to file their complaints online, receive a tracking number and check on the status of a complaint at any time. Complaints are sent first to a complaints officer. If this person fails to resolve the problem within a stipulated time (three days at most), the complaint auto-matically escalates to a higher office and finally to an additional municipal commissioner. Praja and BMC follow up on unresolved issues. Over 400 people file complaints daily. One can also do so in person, in which case the data is entered into the same system. Funding for the system was provided by some private trusts.

---

[9] Richard Rose, 'Openness, Impersonal Rules and Continuing Accountability: The Inter-net's Prospective Impact on East Asia Governance', Paper prepared for World Bank Seminar at the Asian Institute of Harvard University, Anmough Caugen, Massachusetts, 1–2 October 2001.

As is illustrated by OPEN, providing the ability to track the processing of an application for a service (those that are not delivered across the counter) by citizens can increase transparency. If such an ability is available with the supervisors, that can also help in reducing speed money.

Table 3.3 provides some more examples where e-government applications have helped to reduce corruption in the public sector. Although these examples indicate the potential of e-government in tackling corruption, it would be fair to conclude that its overall exploitation has been quite limited. Many applications have been able to build an efficient (less time to transact) service delivery system, but only a few have succeeded in tackling corruption. One of the few examples where the primary focus was on reducing corruption was to introduce online counselling for teachers in Karnataka (see Box 3.4). E-government needs to be seen as one of the many tools to combat corruption and should be implemented as a part of a wider programme for tackling corruption (see Case 7.11 on OPEN).

Table 3.3

Combating Corruption through E-Government

Impact on corruption	*Examples from around the world*	*How does e-government help?*
Reduction of bribes		
	OPEN: Seoul's anti-corruption project Korea (Case 7.11)	Ability to track the processing of an application for a service (those that are not delivered across the counter) by citizens has increased transparency. Supervisors can also track unusual behaviour and collect citizen feedback on corruption
	Philippine customs reform (Case 7.8)	Removes face-to-face contact of inspectors and cargo agents by introducing electronic submission
	Bhoomi: Karnataka, India (Case 7.1)	Takes away discretion to delay or deny by automating the process; keeping a traceable electronic record of transactions reduces

(Table 3.3 contd.)

(Table 3.3 contd.)

Impact on corruption	Examples from around the world	How does e-government help?
		the opportunity for corrupt practices and increases accountability of public officials
Reduction of powerful brokers		
	CARD, Department of Registration, Andhra Pradesh, India (Case 7.3)	Makes procedures simple and transparent; reduces processing time; removes gatekeeping role
Raising public awareness		
	CVC web site, India (Case 7.12)	Names of corrupt officials; performance of prosecuting agencies becomes public
	CRISTAL, Argentina (see Box 3.2)	Details of budget and expenditure at a disaggregate level become public
Transparency and accountability		
	E-procurement in Chile, Mexico, Brazil (Case 7.7)	Makes decisions of selecting a supplier transparent; citizens can analyse public procurement quantity and prices; increases competition by expanding the marketplace to allow for more companies to participate in the bidding process
	Teachers' transfers in Karnataka (see Box 3.4)	Makes rules for prioritising requests transparent

Box 3.4
Teachers' Transfers in Karnataka, India

The Department of Public Instruction in Karnataka has introduced a new system of effecting the transfer of teachers. Every year 15,000 teachers working in government schools request to be transferred to a place of their choice. The process of handling these requests is riddled with corruption and nepotism. In the manual system every teacher seeking a transfer used to submit an application to the administrative controlling authority, the state-level authority and also forward another application through politicians known to the person. Often action was initiated at different points, resulting in multiple transfer orders. Guidelines for processing transfers were not outlined. District authorities were unable to keep track of vacant posts in the district as transfer orders were issued at various levels. Exodus of teachers from backward districts created serious manpower crisis in schools. The need-based distribution of manpower within the district was also disturbed. The system also gave room to a lot of human interference, corruption and harassment for the hapless teachers.

Teacher transfers were streamlined in 2001 by automating the entire process. Under this system, the transfer requests were prioritised based on the 'reasons' cited for a transfer. After long deliberations with teachers and officers at various levels, the priority for each reason was determined. Applicants with reasons such as 'terminally ill', 'suffering from serious illness', 'physically handicapped', 'spouse in government service', 'verge of retirement' and 'working in the same place for more than seven years' were given priority in that order.

All transfer aspirants were instructed to apply to the concerned district authority in a pre-defined format. A computer-generated list containing the names of transfer aspirants along with their ranking (based on their reasons for transfer) was published on the notice-board of the department, and objections if any were invited. By doing so, the whole method became very transparent. During counselling, the teachers were called in order of priority and were allowed to select the place of posting from among the vacant teacher posts in the database. Once the selection was made, a transfer order was printed and handed over and his/her current place of posting was added to the database. Since the vacancy positions were announced in advance, the teachers could make a decision on the place of posting prior to the counselling session. The entire session, including the printing of the transfer order, took around 2 to 5 minutes. This enabled the counselling of seventy-five to 100 teachers on a daily basis. After every session a list of new postings and another list containing vacant positions are published.

Source: Write-up provided by Lakshmisa S., Senior System Analyst, National Informatics Centre Education Unit, Government of Karnataka, India.

Corruption often reflects the power distance between the civil servants and the citizens, particularly in case of poor, illiterate and ignorant citizens in remote areas. Demand for a bribe even when no favour is involved can not be easily refused (as in the case of truckers without overload in the border checkpost case). It is important to supervise and monitor the performance of newly installed e-government systems until the norms of higher levels of service get ingrained in civil servants.

3.2 Improved Service Delivery: Making Services Work for People

E-government helps in reducing the cost incurred by the poor for obtaining services from government agencies. Citizens need to spend less effort in finding out how a service can be obtained because such information is available on web sites (such as publishing rules and procedures). Services can be delivered at the doorstep except where a physical transaction (for example, immunisation) is involved. We have already noted that corruption can be reduced and accountability is enhanced. It also provides greater access to information. Citizens have better documentation for follow-up action. Quick processing time reduces the total time to transact and reduces waiting periods. Fewer visits to government departments are involved.

E-government also makes the delivery system more efficient by introducing competition amongst delivery channels and departments. By automating routine clerical work, staff time is released for more substantive tasks. E-government usually centralises data that can improve audit as it enables unbiased sampling for audit purposes. Integration of data across applications provides improved intelligence. Standardised documentation of comments/objections raised by staff on applications for licences leads to effective supervision. Supervisors have comparative indicators from staff and can determine if a staff is resorting to wilful obstruction. E-government usually provides an entry point for simplification of rules and re-engineering processes (see Case 7.8). Services can also become more effective as ICTs provide the ability to profile clients to tailor services to their specific needs, much like micro-marketing in e-commerce (see Box 3.5).

Box 3.5
India Health Care Project

The basic health care delivery system in India is implemented through primary health centres (PHCs) employing female outreach workers called auxiliary nurse midwives (ANM), each covering a population of 5,000. These ANMs deliver health care to rural people at their homes and maintain a number of records in registers. In a pilot, personal digital assistants (PDAs) were provided to 459 ANMs based in sixty-seven PHCs in Nalgonda district of Andhra Pradesh state for capturing data at the doorsteps of the rural people.

Now ANMs capture and update data in PDAs, completely eliminating the maintenance of multiple paper registers. Nearly 30 per cent of an ANM's time spent on record keeping is now released for fieldwork and improved planning. Data from all PDAs is uploaded to the PHC computer to generate a variety of MIS reports. The PDAs can generate activity plans such as reminders for immunisation, ante- and post-natal care for pregnant women, and distribution of contraceptives. The schedules help the ANM know which households she needs to visit. With the training that was provided, ANMs have not had any problems in using the PDAs. Effectiveness of services has improved. For example, in treating a high-risk pregnant woman, history of past treatment and allergies proves to be very useful.

In a longer time frame, e-government can subtly shift the balance of power between the service providers and clients. In many countries e-government has made governments more citizen centric. Several portals organise information and services according to client needs (such as the Singapore government) and not according to government department structure. E-applications enable greater participation of citizens, leading to their empowerment. For example, it is easy to strengthen feedback on services; collection of statistics on performance in service delivery also becomes easy. This data can also be made public.

Many projects have demonstrated impressive efficiency gains in terms of cutting the number of steps involved, cutting the timeframe, and reducing the number of agencies that need to be consulted (see Table 3.4).

Table 3.4
Examples of Efficiency Gains

Country	Type of govern-ment application	Number of days to process before application	Number of days to process after application
Brazil	Registration of 29 documents	Several days	20–30 minutes per document, one day for business licences
Chile	Taxes online	25 days	12 hours
China	Online application for 32 business services	2–3 months for business licences	10–15 days for business licences
		Several visits to multiple offices for filings	Several seconds for routine filing for companies
India (Andhra Pradesh)	Valuation of property	Few days	10 minutes
India (Andhra Pradesh)	Land registration	7–15 days	5 minutes
India (Andhra Pradesh)	Statutory certifi-cates on caste	20–30 days	15 minutes
India (Karnataka)	Updating land registration	1–2 years	30 days for approval, request completed on demand
India (Karnataka)	Obtaining land title certificates	3–30 days	5–30 minutes
India (Gujarat)	Interstate check-posts for trucks	30 minutes	2 minutes
Jamaica	Customs online	2–3 day for brokers to process entry	3–4 hours
Philippines	Customs online	8 days to release cargo	4 hours to 2 days to release cargo
Singapore	Issue of tax assessments	12–18 months	3–5 months

3.3 Empowerment of Rural Communities

A large number of pilot projects in which rural Internet kiosks have been opened in Asia, Africa and Latin America have not been completely successful in terms of their economic viability.[10] The Gyandoot case study (Case 7.2) presents a pioneering effort to run rural tele-centres with private partnership. The following conclusions can be drawn from Gyandoot and several rural tele-centre projects implemented in other parts of the world:[11]

- Rural populations are willing to pay a fee for systems that have very clear business or personal uses.
- Villagers are not enamoured of electronic delivery. The uptake depends on whether significant value is being delivered in comparison with existing ways of receiving information and services.
- Intermediaries are often needed to respond to the specific information needs of rural citizens, and to interpret and disseminate knowledge from public documents.
- Poor telecom and power infrastructure in rural areas can affect the economic viability of rural kiosks.

Figure 3.1 consolidates this learning. It illustrates that there are four necessary conditions that need to be fulfilled for effective service delivery and bridging the digital divide to empower rural communities. Only a few e-government projects targeted towards rural communities incorporate all the four elements outlined above. Bhoomi (Case 7.1) describes a pilot to create rural tele-centres in which at least three of the above elements are present.

[10] See cases on the Drishtee Telecentre Initiative, http://poverty.worldbank.org/library/view/14646/, and 'E-Chaupal: ITCs Rural Networking Project', http://poverty.worldbank.org/library/view/14647/.

[11] S. Senthilkumaran and Subiah Arunachalam, 'Expanding the Village Knowledge Centres in Pondicherry', *Regional Development Dialog*, Vol. 23, No. 2, 2002, pp. 65–81; Florence Etta, Ramata Aw. Thioune with Edith Adera, Case Study of Acacia Tele-centres: Senegal and Uganda', *Regional Development Dialog*, Vol. 23, No. 2, 2002, pp. 85–101.

Figure 3.1
The Four Pillars for Bridging the Digital Divide

Technology that makes rural access inexpensive and robust

Applications that draw a large clientele that pays for the service, ensuring economic viability of the kiosk

Bridging the digital divide

NGOs and grassroots organisations that catalyse and manage the community building process

Content that empowers rural citizens and enables formation of communities

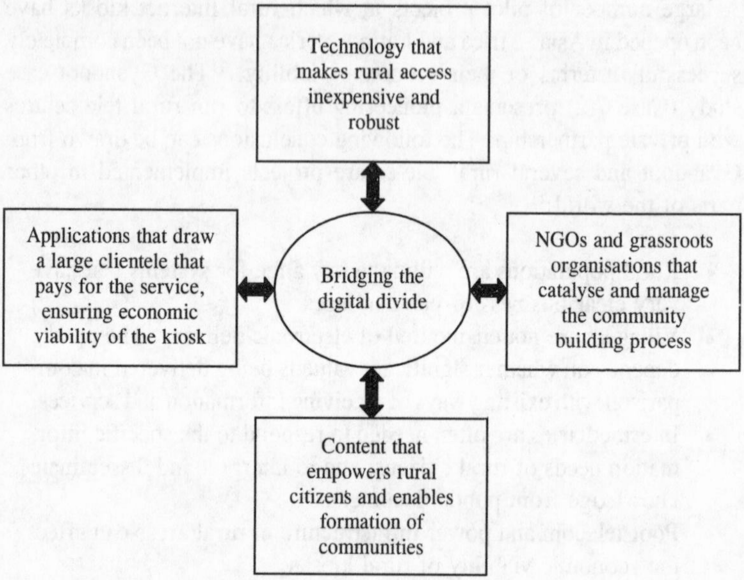

3.4 Gender Focus of E-Government Projects

ICT-led service delivery is expected to radically improve the delivery of social services to the poor. Do the service planners and deliverers keep women at the centre of their service design and delivery efforts? For example, in the delivery of health services, are there special programmes geared to women's needs? Will ICT serve large number of women, generate greater awareness among women about child and health care, improve the mobility, reach or effectiveness of the ANMs who deliver the medical and extension services to poor women? Do e-government initiatives view women as a special category of service recipients with unique needs and preferences? An equally important concern is political empowerment.

Electronic delivery of services by governments is largely confined to regulatory agencies, such as issue of certificates, licences and tax collection. There are very few examples of e-government where health and education services are being delivered through the use of ICT. In most of these examples there is little focus on content that is especially useful for women or on services that are primarily used by women. A pilot application in Andhra Pradesh is an exception where ANMs use PDAs to record service data on mother and child health care and family planning. The use of PDAs makes the task of the ANMs less burdensome, increases efficiency in data collection and storage, and streamlines the actual delivery of services (see Box 3.5).

In Gyandoot (Case 7.2) there was no special effort directed to benefit women, but the project succeeded in helping a few rural women in its first year. For example, widows in villages could send e-mails at negligible cost to the local bureaucracy to put pressure regarding payment of pensions that had not been paid for several months. Small-town women traders could check the latest market prices for their products through the computer so that they were no longer at the mercy of middlemen.

Most e-government applications are of recent origin and have not been evaluated in detail to determine whether they promote greater use of services by women. FRIENDS in Kerala (Case 7.5) is an exception. It provides one-stop service centres to collect all kinds of payments made to government agencies, including utility bills, university fees and licence fees. An evaluation of the project in 2002 showed that the number of women making such payments at the FRIENDS service centres was more (11.3 per cent) than the number of women making similar payments at 74 departmental counters (3.1 per cent). Eighty per cent of women respondents indicated a preference for using the FRIENDS centre. Whether this helps women in any particular way is difficult to state.

In some cases of e-government, women have emerged as unintended beneficiaries. For example, in Brazil's efforts to provide e-government services in rural areas of Bahia, women happen to gain most from the visits of the mobile Assistance Service Centre (SAC) unit because men migrate to cities to seek employment and women constitute the predominant rural population.[12] The SAC is a large truck equipped with a computer and other facilities to provide birth certificates, identification cards, labour identification cards and criminal record verification to the rural community at their doorstep. It remains parked near a rural community for a few days before moving to the next rural area.

Examples of conscious incorporation of women-friendly policies and practices in e-government are almost non-existent. In social service

[12] For more details of the project see the case study at http://www1.worldbank.org/publicsector/egov/bahiaSAC.htm.

delivery, women are recipients of benefits arising from the use of ICT, especially through services such as health and education. Being passive beneficiaries of these services, women have little power to influence the use of ICT. It is necessary, therefore, that these services are designed and implemented keeping in mind the special requirements, convenience and preferences of women. E-government projects meant to benefit women can succeed, provided women are consulted and involved both at the design and implementation stages, and their concerns and requirements are addressed through the project.

3.5 Economic Goals: Reducing Costs and Increasing Revenues

There are several areas where e-government can have potential economic impact. E-government can increase the competitiveness of a nation by reducing the costs of setting up and operating an enterprise. The costs of setting up an enterprise can be reduced by making the process of business registration, issue of a variety of licences and provision of services fast, efficient and corruption free. Corruption adds significantly to the cost of doing business and any lowering of corruption can make the industry more competitive through simplification of government rules and procedures and by increasing transparency in their implementation, governments can reduce some amount of uncertainty for the investor. As we noted in chapter 2, the primary objective of some governments in implementing e-government is to enhance their image of being investor friendly.

E-government can make a significant impact on government finances. Leakage in government revenues can be plugged by making tax collection services efficient (with incentives for tax payers to comply), providing tools for improved audit of likely defaulters and evaders, and reducing collusion between tax payers and collection agencies by minimising opportunities for corruption.

In most countries, public procurement, the letting of contracts for major public works and the sale of public assets are the sources of so-called grand corruption, sometimes resulting in huge losses for the government. For example, in a number of countries hoodlums may be employed by bidders to prevent competitors from delivering their bids to the designated public tendering office, sometimes with the connivance of the police and officials concerned. Such problems can be overcome by instituting arrangements for delivering bids via the Internet as has been done successfully in Chile, Mexico and Brazil. These e-procurement systems save cost of advertising requirements, lower prices of procurement through more competition, and reduce the cost of paper work within procurement agencies and at the supplier end (see Case 7.7 on e-procurement implementation).

Pilfering of public stores and the theft of public property can result in huge financial losses. The use of bar codes to track inventory can enable such losses to be quickly noted and the culprits more easily identified. The issue of illegal logging fits into this category. Vast sums are involved in forest corruption. A number of organisations have been experimenting with the use of bar codes to enable the origin and legitimacy of log consignments to be checked along the marketing chain. If there is effective commitment by relevant officials anywhere along that chain, illegal logs can be confiscated, providing a strong incentive to those engaged in the timber trade to be honest and to insist that those upstream respect the requirements for sustainable forest management. Because the bar coded information is stored on computer networks and widely shared, there is an increased transparency that deters fraudsters.

Transparent and efficient delivery of services connected with economic activity can stimulate production growth by correcting the incentive structure. For example, a fair payment system for the procurement of milk and farm produce in rural areas, and removal of intermediaries from the procurement process can provide the incentive for increasing investments in productive resources and improving yields.[13]

Improving service delivery to citizens helps increase all-round productivity by diminishing time wasted in commuting, standing in queues and seeking information. Three of these areas are explored further.

Cost Reduction in Service Delivery

Although many applications in developing countries have shown significant benefits in general, cost reduction has not taken place. In most

---

[13] R. Chakravarty, 'IT at Milk Collection Centres at Cooperative Dairies: The National Dairy Development Board Experience' in S.C. Bhatnagar and Robert Schware (eds), *Information and Communication Technology in Development: Cases From India*. New Delhi: Sage Publications, 2000.

cases e-government becomes an additional channel to offer services. Even in developed countries where Internet penetration is high, the proportion of citizens using a portal for services is low. Until this proportion reaches a level so that there can be some cutback in the number of personnel employed in delivering services through the traditional departmental channel or telephone, there will be little reduction in costs. In fact, initially the costs will rise on account of investments in organising electronic delivery. In developed countries privacy and security issues seem to be holding the citizens back. This problem has not surfaced in developing countries as the Internet penetration is very low.

Without a critical mass using the application, particularly for revenue-generating applications such as taxes or fee-based services, cost recovery does not seem promising. However, experience has shown that even rural poor citizens are willing to pay a reasonable fee for a useful service. There are a few examples, such as the Bhoomi project in Karnataka (see Case 7.1), where farmers pay a transaction fee of Rs 15 for receiving a signed copy of a land title from an online kiosk. In the first year 5.5 million farmers have collected titles, forking out nearly Rs 80 million, which is half the cost of the entire project.

Control of Government Expenditure

E-government can also help governments in expenditure control. Many countries have implemented integrated financial management systems (IFMS)[14] to track and control payments made out of government treasuries. For example, the state of Karnataka has connected all its 216 treasuries through a satellite-based network (see Box 3.6). Every payment is now centrally authenticated to ensure that a budget provision exists for the payment and that it is not exceeded. Such systems focus on expenditure control, not exploiting the full potential of the system to combat corruption and improve service delivery. Experience suggests that it is difficult to implement IFMS as they are complex and need to be comprehensive in their scope to deliver concrete benefits.

---

[14] Bill Dorotinsky, 'Integrated Financial Management System: An Important but Limited Anti-Corruption Tool', http://www1.worldbank.org/publicsector/egov/anticoregovseminar/bill%20transprency%20and%20ifms.doc.

Box 3.6
Khajane, Karnataka, India

In the Indian state of Karnataka, the treasury system handles payment of over Rs 200 billion annually. The system serves around 18 million pensioners, the physically handicapped and destitute widows. The treasuries act as bankers to 4,500 panchayats,[15] municipal corporations and other funds. The manual system has been susceptible to various kinds of frauds. For instance, in places where there are only six staff members on the rolls, departments were drawing salaries for ten to twelve employees. Sometimes allocated money for specific projects was overdrawn. The Khajane (treasuries) initiative involving the computerisation of all the treasuries in Karnataka aims at bringing transparency and accountability in the system of financial transactions and also discipline in operations and management, resulting in efficiency and cost savings for the government.

All 216 treasuries have been connected to the Network Management Centre (NMC), the main database centre located in Bangalore via VSAT (Very Small Aperture Terminal) links. A disaster recovery centre has been created in another location. Signatures of all the 27,100 drawing and disposing officers are captured online. About 2,000 treasuries' employees have been given basic computer training. Another 600 have been trained in hardware and application software. In addition, seventy-five have been trained in system administration. The total project cost stands between Rs 320 and 350 million.

The Khajane software can track bills and pinpoint where a bill is pending and who is the officer in charge. The transactions are much faster now. Pensioners and NGOs can be paid every month instead of every two months. Every payment made at any treasury is now authorised centrally based on a test of 671 parameters. The whole process takes a few seconds. The system's benefits include:

- Total control of the budget for all government departments, 4,500 panchayats and municipal corporations. Khajane monitors stocks for stamps and safe custody articles in the state.
- Elimination of fraud or duplication of data entry.
- Financial control. The system provides regular updates regarding state expenditure and receipts to the central server.

Source: 'Khajane: Linking Treasuries, E-Governance: The South Gets Serious', http://www.express-computer.com/20021028/bangalore3.shtml.

[15] Local self-governments at the village, the sub-sub-district and the district levels.

Another strategy to control expenditure is to introduce paper-less offices in large government departments. Few of these applications have been implemented. The SmartGov project (Case 7.10) in Andhra Pradesh is an example where the entire state secretariat is being made paper-less. The more potent savings through downsizing of governments has not yet happened, however, because of the strong resistance from well-organised unions of government employees.

Growth of Tax Revenue

The inefficient collection of taxes in many developing countries has led to cash-strapped governments that are incapable of enforcing payments. Moreover, corruption in the collection process leads to less money going to the government and lack of public confidence in the system. Modernising tax systems through e-government applications has been a priority for many countries. Through online tax filing and processing systems, governments aim to reduce corruption and enhance transparency to create more public trust. Chile has been able to reach significant savings through their online tax system. With over 400,000 taxpayers checking their assessments and 200,000 submitting taxes online, the government had begun to see significant cost savings and increased accuracy. The Chilean exchequer has collected almost $2 billion through the electronic system (for details, see Case 7.6).

Computerised interstate checkposts in Gujarat, India, have resulted in a three-fold increase in tax collection over two years. Revenue increased from $12 million to $50 million, paying back the total project cost of $34 million in just six months (see Case 7.9).

The scope of e-government as it is implemented today is not wide enough to have generated a macro-level impact that is discernible through aggregate indicators. Investments in e-government are relatively small to have created such a macro impact.

4

Guidelines for Implementing Projects Successfully

Some valuable lessons have emerged through the case studies, which provide important considerations for governments in developing countries as they begin to implement e-government projects. There are three main delivery models that have emerged. Agency departments are going online, without waiting for direction from above. To provide maximum outreach, governments are investing in conveniently located service centres. Increasingly, governments are creating one-stop shop portals[1] to increase self-service options for citizens and businesses.

4.1 Defining a Project Scope: Starting Small

One of the key factors is an appropriate definition of the scope of the project. Given the versatile nature of information technology, there are many different tasks that an e-government application can perform. However, making the scope of a project very ambitious from the beginning increases the risk of failure in implementation. Often a large-scope project involves a very large number of stakeholders who are affected by the application. Managing such large-scale change proves to be difficult. Some ambitious projects are based on untested technology (such as GIS[2]

---

[1] One-stop shop portals offer citizens services of numerous departments through one portal. In effect, it eliminates the need to browse through a maze of departmental web sites to reach a service or piece of information. Current one-stop shop portals include the UK Government Info and Services Online (ukonline.gov) and Government of Canada Online.

[2] A Geographical Information System (GIS) uses information from many different sources, in many different forms. The primary requirement for the data is that the locations for the variables are known. Location may be any variable that can be located spatially and can be fed into a GIS. Several computer databases that can be directly entered into a GIS are being produced by government agencies and private firms.

and smart card),[3] which can lead to failure. The example of computerisation of interstate checkposts in Gujarat (Case 7.9) illustrates how use of untested technology can lead to project failure. It is very important for these projects to focus on measurable goals in terms of the specific benefits that would be delivered to citizens, businesses or government employees depending on the nature of the application. An example of computerisation of property registration in Andhra Pradesh (Case 7.3) demonstrates the value of being focused on measurable goals.

Pilot projects have allowed governments to experiment and tailor their product to fit the needs of users. The safest approach to adopting a new technology with a steep learning curve is to take small steps with activities that are manageable within a relatively short time-frame. This allows greater flexibility for tailoring the system and formulating a long-term strategy based on the actual experiences of the organisation and feedback from the client. If capable of showing quick success, pilot projects allow for buy-in from groups that are originally resistant. Bhoomi (Case 7.1) illustrates the advantage of using a phased approach in defining project scope.

4.2 Designing a Citizen-centric Service Delivery Mechanism

There are a number of tasks such as acquiring information about government rules and procedures, applying for permits and licences, and obtaining legal documents for which citizens interact with government. Traditionally, for most of these tasks, citizens had to make several trips to a departmental counter. A very limited amount of information is available over the phone. Community service centres (offering electronic delivery of multiple services) and a web site are the new channels for delivering such information and services.

When alternate channels are available, uptake of a new one like a web portal is slow. Significant effort and resources need to be spent to make citizens aware of the added advantages that Internet channels can offer as opposed to traditional one. This is particularly true in projects like Gyandoot (Case 7.2) and Bhoomi (Case 7.1), which serve rural

---

Different kinds of data in map form can be entered into a GIS. For example, digital satellite images can be analysed to produce a map-like layer of digital information.

[3] The term Smart Card is used to describe any card with a capability to relate information to a particular application such as magnetic stripes, optical memory and microprocessor cards.

populations. The number of access points have to be sufficient to be within easy reach, and citizens also need to be trained to navigate through service delivery portals. Local language interfaces need to be built. Countries with significant illiterate populations have to create access points where assistance is provided. Intermediaries such as volunteers/kiosk owners/paid employees often play a positive role in applications where information is disseminated to rural/illiterate populations.[4]

The design of the web site is critical. It should be simple to search for information and the information should be complete. Citizens should not have to follow up a web site access with a visit or a call. If several departments have web sites, then there should be a common look and feel, which minimises learning on the part of the citizen. The information delivered to a citizen through all the media (a web site, telephone, office visit or as paper documents) should be consistent. Often procedures are modified, but such modification is not reflected in every channel that a citizen can access.

To make a web site useful, it is critical that time is invested in building appropriate content. Designing web sites is a demanding task and should be done by professionals. Many successful portals are seen to be citizen centric because they follow a navigation structure that closely mimics the life cycle of a citizen.[5] It needs to factor in the quality of Internet infrastructure available in the country so that down load times can be kept within acceptable limits. Standards need to be laid down for look and feel, data definitions, structures of databases, security provisions and an organisational structure to maintain the integrity of data.

4.3 How Much to Automate

E-government does not require that all the steps in the delivery of a service should be handled electronically. Handling a few of the critical components electronically can derive significant benefits. For example, in Chile, the e-procurement system announces the requirements of the

[4] In Sri Lanka the existence of volunteers who run the Kothmale community radio has contributed to the success of the programme. The daily programme received an average of five to six queries for which volunteers seek information from the Internet and then broadcast the responses. See 'Kothmale Community Radio/Internet Project: Expanding the Knowledge Base', http://www1.worldbank.org/publicsector/egov/kothmale_cs.htm.

[5] The best example of such a portal is SINGOV: Singapore Government Online Portal, http://www.gov.sg.

government on a web site, but handles the bids in a manual mode. Registered suppliers for the needed product/service are sent an e-mail to broaden the choice of suppliers. Once the bids have been processed manually, the results are announced electronically on a web site. Significant costs have been saved in Chile because of expanded supplier choice. In addition, the whole process of selection of suppliers has been made more transparent. Yet the core process of bidding continues to be manual (see Case 7.7). There are many examples where some components of an electronic service delivery continue to be handled manually. Yet in all these examples significant benefits have been delivered to the users in terms of reduced time and less corruption.

In environments where ICT infrastructure is non-existent, departments may choose to aim for partial instead of complete electronic delivery (see FRIENDS implementation in Case 7.4). The extent of automation is also determined by the need to reduce the discretion available to civil servants in processing transactions. Complete automation can reduce the gatekeeper role that many officers play in manual systems. It can also prevent arbitrary action of delaying service to some customers or expediting services to others who pay speed money.

The benefits delivered from such hybrid applications are substantial compared to traditional methods of service delivery. Benefits of moving from these hybrid solutions to a fully automated self-service mode may not be commensurate with the additional investments that are needed.

4.4 Avoid Reinventing the Wheel

Often rules and procedures that govern the delivery of a particular type of service are not standardised across countries. Therefore, packaged solutions are available only in a few application domains. The advantage of off-the-shelf solutions is that the software is tried and tested. In applications that deal with procurement and customs, there are a number of generic solutions that only need marginal tailoring for local conditions. ASYCUDA[6] is one such example (Box 4.1).

[6] ASYCUDA is a computerised customs management system, which covers most foreign trade procedures. The system handles manifests and customs declarations, accounting procedures, transit and suspense procedures. ASYCUDA can be configured to suit the national characteristics of individual customs regimes and national tariff legislation. ASYCUDA provides for electronic data interchange (EDI) between traders and customs using Electronic Data Interchange for Administration, Commerce and Transport (EDIFACT) rules.

Box 4.1

ASYCUDA: Avoid Reinventing the Wheel

Online processing of imports/exports in customs departments is an excellent example of benefits from the use of standard software. ASYCUDA designed by UNCTAD has been used in nearly sixty countries to computerise processing of exports/imports at airports and seaports. The time for implementation has been shortened and it has been easy to implement the system in countries like Yemen, which lack local capacity in developing software. Presumably, ASYCUDA has been designed after studying best practices in different countries. It offers readymade templates for re-engineering processes to increase efficiency, reduce processing time, and make self-assessment and selective audit. The physical contact between the customs inspector and a cargo handling agent has been eliminated. These tools have a significant impact in reducing corruption in customs transactions.

It may be worthwhile for designers to scout for core ideas around which successful applications have been built. One such idea is to introduce payments linked to automated weighing machines. For example, in Calcutta the system of municipal waste collection by private contractors has been computerised. The weight of lorries entering and leaving landfill sites is recorded electronically and the cheques in payment due at the end of each month are generated automatically. There is no opportunity for the operators to 'negotiate' the payments; the result has been a 30 per cent saving to the municipality in the cost of garbage collection. Some of these benefits have been shared with the operators in an equitable way, thereby providing legitimate rewards for good performance. A similar idea was used in the case of interstate checkposts in Gujarat where fine collection is based on the weight of trucks. Another example of use of this idea is milk collection centres in dairies in India at 3,000 rural locations.

4.5 Process Re-engineering

Many e-government applications are implemented in a quick time-frame, which does not permit the re-engineering of processes. When online systems are implemented it is difficult to make changes subsequently. Therefore, it is a good practice to limit the scope of the application (services covered) to contain the effort to a planned level while maintaining an emphasis on the depth of re-engineering that needs to be conducted.

Re-engineering administrative processes and re-organisation of information ownership is the most important step for implementing an e-government application. Many task managers of e-government projects have noted that a large percentage of time is spent in change management and process re-engineering.

Process re-engineering requires that an agency implement substantive reform in organisational structure, initiate a change in culture and mindset, train and improve skills of its people, and put in place the appropriate supporting ICT infrastructure to enable online processes that are timely and efficient to both the user and the government agency. The process or transaction fundamentally changes to allow the efficiency and transparency gains associated with e-government. While these tasks need not happen simultaneously, they need to be in place before an e-government application is offered to the public so that immediate impact and value can be acquired.

The task of re-engineering begins with mapping of existing methods and procedures.[7] Often different branches of the same department do not use the same procedures as local context and conditions result in variations being introduced over time. Existing procedures need to be simplified in a manner that the overall task can be completed in as few steps as possible without compromising on the basic purposes. Often tasks are carried out in a mechanical fashion because with time the original purpose of carrying out these tasks has been lost or forgotten. Government agencies must evaluate every step in the processing cycle to ascertain if it adds any value. If a process is not serving a purpose that is valid, it should be eliminated. This entire process of simplification of documents and workflow, points of approval and audit is termed as re-engineering. Such re-engineering must precede any exercise in automation.

The outcome of re-engineering may be to modify processes, resulting in fewer steps and limiting the number of people needed to perform the tasks. This has a significant effect on the way that civil servants perform

---

[7] According to the BPR Online Learning Centre, business process re-engineering, referred to as re-engineering in this paper, is the redesign of business processes and the associated systems and organisational structures to achieve a dramatic improvement in performance. BPR is not downsizing, restructuring, reorganisation, automation or new technology (definition from http://www.prosci.com/reengineering.htm).

tasks and can produce a considerable resistance from the mid to lower levels of civil servants. A great challenge in implementing e-government is to overcome this resistance through education and training. E-government projects have to consciously strive to provide benefits to civil servants at this level, as they are the ones that tend to lose power and authority over citizens when electronic delivery of services is introduced. E-government projects need to focus on making the entire process of decisions making more transparent. Because of automation, the workflow is regulated and often civil servants lose the flexibility to deal with applications in any sequence other than the one dictated by the computerisation. This takes away the power of patronage and inability to expedite work as in the case of Bhoomi (Case 7.1) and the computerisation of customs (Case 7.8). On the other hand, inability to stall work can be noticed easily because both the public and the supervisors now have the capacity to track information and application as they move from workstation to workstation.

Successful implementation of projects requires that there is a clear focus on the purpose for which the application is being built, as is illustrated by the project on computerising property registration in Andhra Pradesh (Case 7.3). The intended beneficiaries of the application are identified and benefits that will accrue to the stakeholders are concretised. In fact, specific benefits like reduction in time or number of trips to an office need to be targeted and made public. It is only then that the process of re-engineering can work towards its ultimate goal.

Typically, e-government requires complete back-end computerisation and integration for workflow and data sharing. This allows for seamless information sharing and reorganisation of information ownership. Many e-government projects remain limited or fail as a result of neglecting this process. There have been a few examples of successful improvement of services without computerising the back end.[8] The FRIENDS project (Case 7.4) is one such example.

---

[8] An exceptional case is the example of Bahia, Brazil, which was able to successfully roll out e-government services without going through this process. Through citizen service centres, Brazilians in Bahia were able to acquire multiple government services in one location. Over half the workforce for the centres were made up of new contract employees who provided services to citizens at a service centre. Similarly, Poupatempo 'Time Saver' Citizen Centres in Brazil provided citizens with government services without significant re-engineering of the back-end processes. The citizen centres improved the image of the government because the model was perceived as a 'modern' high-quality system for providing public services.

4.6 Capacity to Manage Change

Many e-government projects face substantial resistance from internal staff. Public servants view e-government projects as a threat to their jobs. E-government changes workload, work profile and work content. It forces the need for retooling and training. It often creates redundancy of employees. Public servants see the automation of a process as a loss of power and responsibility. When information is published and easily accessed, they view this as a loss of control. Their role as an intermediary between citizen and government is minimised.

E-government effects civil service in several ways. It alters accountability, reduces discretion and flexibility, and makes performance monitorable and visible. Often e-government forces information sharing and provides easier and equal access to organisational knowledge to all employees. Even citizens become privy to some part of the information. It tends to flatten hierarchy (alters the power and authority vested at different levels). Different groups in the civil service may be affected differently. Some effects may increase resistance to change, whereas others may accelerate acceptance of change. Introduction of a paperless environment in SmartGov (Case 7.10) illustrates many of these effects.

Fear of Unknown Introduces Resistance

This may happen because of introduction of new technology, changes in procedures and different work assignment. Uncertainty in benefits that may accrue from the new system or a perception that disadvantages outweigh advantages for individuals can also lead to resistance.

Attitudinal Factors

The perception that someone else will get the credit for the success of the system can also create resistance in the higher echelons of civil service. Design of the application needs to be reviewed for increase in workload, the need for new learning as some processes are changed, and introduction of complexity in some tasks. Technical performance such as poor access, lack of bandwidth, down time, slow response, frequent breakdowns and software problems can also build resistance.

Effects on civil service need to be understood and mapped into accelerating (making it easier to implement) and decelerating factors. Strategies need to devised to dampen deceleration and enhance acceleration. We have already discussed many actions that help minimise resistance. Some known generic strategies are discussed.

Ensure that the organisational climate is right. By ensuring shared values with advocates of change, a sense of ownership can be generated amongst employees. Participative design where employees' feedback and involvement helps shape the new initiative/process/system can contribute to greater acceptance. Quality of work life and job satisfaction need to be seen as explicit objectives in the design of the new initiative. Training and education of all levels of employees can help mitigate fear of the unknown and reduce resistance.

Ensure all stakeholders understand the expected pay-off, and the role of stakeholders in terms of new tasks and development of skills. Counselling is often a useful mechanism. It is also necessary to gather stakeholder feedback on their understanding of these changes.

Change has to be explicitly managed and, therefore, needs an organisation. Some useful mechanisms are to identify champions and legitimise their role. There needs to be a clear definition of a project team and a command structure. For encouraging a participative design, user-led design groups have to be organised.

Identifying obstacles to change in advance of implementation is important as it helps in defining strategies to overcome obstacles. These obstacles may be financial, technical, organisational, social or the presence of anti-champions.

A large part of the implementation effort, some say up to 40 per cent, must be spent on managing change. For a project leader it is important to garner political support for the proposed project. It is critical that support is demonstrated publicly through workshops and seminars organised for employees. The project must build benefits for all stakeholders. Training helps to alleviate anxiety amongst employees about changes in methods of working. Pilot projects enable civil servants to understand exactly what may lie in store, and also to experience the benefits. Project managers need to be trained in managing change.

The property registration project in Andhra Pradesh (Case 7.3) provides an interesting insight into the problem of resistance. The number of local intermediaries who stood to lose from the changes due to the project had to be appeased so that a complete boycott of the project did not occur. The government did not banish the intermediaries by law, but instead allowed the market to eliminate gradually the demand for them. Care was also taken not to antagonise the lower rungs of bureaucracy. The government announced at the outset that no downsizing would result from the introduction of this technology. The project consciously sought to build some benefits for the operating levels of bureaucracy.

4.7 Strong Internal Leadership and Project Management

Strong leadership has been cited as a defining factor for success in all cases. High-level leadership and support from the top levels of government have facilitated buy-in from other government departments. Strong leadership also creates motivation from other agencies to join in the process. Leadership is also important as it helps 'sell' the project to a larger internal audience and the public.

Besides leadership, many governments face lack of adequate human resources to implement and manage projects related to e-government. Strong project management skills are needed within the department. Project managers need to clearly identify goals and benefits in concrete terms. The task is often vast and not manageable within the resources that are available internally to a government department. Many tasks such as design, software development, data preparation and training can easily be outsourced. Systems analysis, which provides the necessary cues for re-engineering, should be conducted internally.

Training expenses should not be minimised. Successful projects typically spend about 10 per cent of the budget on training. Awareness about benefits of e-government has to be created in senior civil servants and political executives. Training is required for project leaders who need to define project deliverables, deal (negotiate) with consultants and vendors, and manage an outsourced development process. Clerical staff need to be trained on specific applications. Supervisors and managers need to be trained on using information. Citizens need to be made aware of online services and how to transact business on web portals. Successful computerisation of land records in Karnataka (Case 7.1) and property registration in Andhra Pradesh (Case 7.3) illustrate the role of leadership and the importance of training.

4.8 Being Prepared for a Slow Ramp Up

There has been a concern, given the cost in using ICT channels, that usage build-up of an e-service would be more gradual than expected when alternate modes of service delivery are available. Although this continues to be a barrier to achieving a critical mass for e-government, some projects have shown that the poor are willing to pay as long as the service delivers value. E-government channels are quickly embraced if the service provided fulfils the needs of the community. Uptake in the Bhoomi project (Case 7.1) in Karnataka was quick because no alternate channel was permitted. Bhoomi issued 5.5 million land titles in the first year of operations. In the SmartGov project in Andhra Pradesh, the number of transactions has crossed the 10-million mark even though competing channels of departmental counters are still open.[9] On the other hand, the number of transactions from the rural Gyandoot project has dwindled to a few hundred as it is not perceived by the public to be delivering value. To create a critical mass of users, a number of e-government projects incorporate activities that raise awareness of targeted users. These include training of service providers and potential users, publicity and media campaigns before, during and after the implementation phase of the project.[10]

5

Guidelines for Designing a Country-wide Strategy for E-Government

5.1 The Need for a Strategy and Implementation Plan

A key issue faced by government officials is how to approach e-government. Should e-government come as the culmination of public sector reforms, preceded by other efforts to rationalise government activity and strengthen key institutions, or can e-government applications serve as a catalyst for such change? Reform of the public sector is typically painful, slow and meets much resistance. The appeal of e-government in developing countries can sometimes overcome resistance to change. In a number of cases e-government applications have been the catalyst for change and have enabled public sector reforms to move quickly. Sequencing of different reform initiatives can be a question of tactics, but for e-government to be effective, it must be implemented in a wider context of basic reforms.

An e-government strategy will encompass answers to many such questions in the specific context of a country. Developing a strategy would require an assessment of the readiness of a country. The strategy will define the nature of projects that are taken up, the organisational and institutional arrangements that can best harness resources and deliver the intended benefits. A policy framework would need to be defined for creating a supportive environment. Most important, the idea of ICT-enabled reform will have to be packaged and sold to different stakeholders such as citizens, civil servants and non-governmental institutions.

5.2 When is a Country Ready?

Some consulting organisations have developed tool kits to assess e-readiness of countries. However, there are very few kits available for assessing e-government readiness.[1] Broadly, e-government readiness would cover the following factors:

1. the extent to which computerisation of back-end processes has been conducted as well as hardware, software and networking infrastructure required to provide access points to clients at the front end;
2. a strong intent to reform governance backed up by demonstrated political will and leadership;
3. capacity to design and implement e-government systems as demonstrated by existence of institutions, which can assist in systems analysis, design, process re-engineering and software development;
4. availability of funds to support the e-government effort;
5. existence of an enabling legal framework encompassing privacy and security of data, legal sanction of new forms of storage and archiving, and laws that accept paperless transactions; and
6. finally, the most important factor is the attitude of the civil servants. Civil servants need to have a customer orientation, willingness to change, adequate ICT literacy, and a modicum of honesty and integrity.

The assessment of e-government readiness has to be based on a mix of quantitative measures and qualitative assessment, which can best be done by appropriately trained consultants through field visits to different departments. No government is completely ready for e-government, but that does not mean that such projects should not be taken up.

5.3 Bottom-up Approach versus Top-down

Some governments have opted for centralised, well-defined and controlled national strategy.[2] Typically, large countries have chosen a

---

[1] 'UNPAN, E-Government Readiness Assessment Methodology', http://www.unpan.org/dpepa-kmb-eg-egovranda-ready.asp.

[2] For example Jordan, Mauritius and Singapore have followed a centrally driven strategy.

more decentralised approach, allowing for bottom-up initiatives, letting individual departments drive their own projects. There are risks and merits to each approach. A bottom-up approach of 'letting a thousand flowers bloom' without any coordination can result in overlap, lack of focus and waste of funds. A centralised approach is difficult to implement because it leaves very little room for innovation, self-starters and creativity, making it hard for buy-in from different departments.

One of the major drawbacks of a bottom-up strategy is the use of a variety of hardware and software platforms by different field agencies. This tends to impede designing systems that allow agencies to share data and transactions across departments, which is necessary integrated or joined up government.[3]

In some countries different departments use their own method of identifying citizens. This leads to a multiplicity of citizen identification cards, causing a problem for the citizen as well as creating confusion within a government, resulting in multiple record keeping of the same information.

In countries that are new to e-government, a bottom-up strategy has been quite popular as this has allowed national agencies, state and municipal governments to launch projects that have quick impact and low risk. Many government departments have implemented such projects without waiting for the adoption of a national strategy or the creation of a coordination unit. Many local governments have seen impressive results because they are well placed to implement small, focused projects that involve low risk.

Perhaps creating a central coordination unit offers the right balance. It promotes better use of resources, reduces overlap and allows for better goals setting. Additionally, it gives enough flexibility for initiatives to be carried out from lower levels of government. Clearly defined guidelines by a central agency for data definitions, hardware/software platforms and citizen identification cards can be very useful in promoting data sharing. Many countries are adopting this approach with varying degrees of coordination and control. Colombia's centrally coordinated approach illustrated in Box 5.1 focused on monitoring and achieved good results. Departmental ownership of e-government is vital because no external agency can drive the kind of change that is needed in

---

[3] 'Joined-up Government' involves new channels and new points of connection (using ICT) between different parts of government in the area of policy making, operations and services.

implementing e-government. The state of Andhra Pradesh is the best example of a centrally coordinated strategy.[4]

Box 5.1
Columbia's Carrot-and-Stick Approach

Columbia opted for a top-down strategy and provided strong leadership with direct involvement from the president. The president established an action framework for ICT development and used both carrots and sticks by ordering government agencies to engage in e-government by creating a web site, offering online services and conducting purchases online by a specific date. The government also provided a carrot by helping agencies to comply with the requirements. The government monitors and publishes the degree of agency compliance on a web site, which has led to healthy competition between agencies.

A centrally coordinated approach can encourage departmental initiative through suitable incentives, and also avoids the pitfalls of a completely bottom-up approach where data sharing is hampered and delivery of services such as licensing for a business, where a large amount of documents and data must be shared across departments, becomes difficult. Also, each department may not have the capacity to use the correct method and latest design techniques in developing the application. A central agency can provide the necessary guidance in use of correct methodology. It can also build and maintain common services that are required to be used by different departments.

Reporting arrangements for such an agency within the government structure can be tricky. Typically, such agencies have been set up as part of the budget/finance ministry or even as part of the civil service reform agency. Such an agency needs a power base that enables it to coordinate work across different agencies. It also needs a home that enables it to attract a multi-disciplinary professional staff. Often e-government projects are viewed as information technology projects, within the sole domain of the information services department, as opposed to an enabler of core business services. This approach has several drawbacks. For

---

[4] S.C. Bhatnagar, 'E-Government: Supporting the Administration for India's States', in Howes, S, A. Lahiri and Nicholas Stern (eds), *State-level Reforms in India: Towards More Effective Government*. New Delhi: Macmillan, 2003, pp. 257–67.

example, it results in low buy-in from the staff that is responsible for providing the service. Consequently, there is lack of change management and business process re-engineering needed for the project to realise the efficiencies associated with e-government.

5.4 Selecting Quick-strike Projects

Quick-strike projects are helpful in demonstrating potential gains from e-government. They allow different stakeholders to understand what e-government holds in store for them. Such projects help in generating demands from citizens for more such initiatives. They enable the implementers and central teams to learn about specific bottlenecks and how these can be tackled. They help in breaking down any organised resistance within civil servants by demonstrating gains and losses for them.

A list of quick-strike projects can be chosen by inviting proposals from different departments. Projects that are typically easier to implement and deliver significant benefits should be chosen. Some governments identify departments that have the maximal contact with citizens/businesses and others choose departments that are perceived to be corrupt and inefficient. Those departments that have already computerised the back end are good candidates as implementation effort is less. Most important is the support for reform from the political and administrative leadership and the presence of a high-energy, innovative civil servant at a senior level to act as a project champion.

Prioritising pilot projects to choose quick-strike projects has been a good practice adopted by many early implementers of e-government. It is often useful to assess the risk and benefits of projects. To prioritise and select projects, many countries have developed a framework for evaluation, allowing them to choose those projects that complemented their priorities with those that demonstrated quick value for the citizen.

The framework provided in Figure 5.1 illustrates a strategy that involves selecting pilot projects by balancing risk in implementation with the perceived value that the project will deliver to beneficiaries. Many government departments with little or no experience in ICT can test the waters by opting for projects in the top bottom quadrant representing low-value, low-risk projects. For example, they can begin by publishing web sites that provide information about rules, procedures and basic information. This generally is low in risk and low in value; however, in some countries where government information is difficult to access,

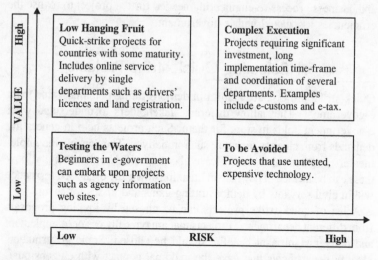

Figure 5.1
Balancing Risk and Value in Selecting Projects

this approach has much value in creating a basic sense of transparency of government information. Low-risk and high-value projects (top left quadrant) are often innovative. Such projects are started by individual departments and target a specific community need, such as the ability to acquire forms online. High-risk, low-value projects (bottom right quadrant) are to be avoided. These often involve initiatives that are untried, untested and can significantly affect the government's credibility if they fail. High-value, high-risk projects (top right quadrant) often provide significant benefit to citizens and businesses and involve services such as the ability to pay online fines, taxes and conduct procurement processes online from bid announcements to final selection. These require complex and long implementation periods and coordination from more than two departments. Many projects aiming at 'joined-up government' fall into this category.

5.5 Public–Private Partnerships and the Role of Government Agencies

Popularly believed to be the fastest and most efficient approach to rolling out e-government services, public–private partnerships are often a key element of an e-government strategy. In the simplest arrangement the private sector is used for outsourcing different components of work in developing an application. In several Indian projects (see Bhoomi [Case 7.1] and CARD [Case 7.3]) software development, training, data entry of manual archives and maintenance have been outsourced to the private sector. Private companies can also be used to develop an e-government application as a product, as was done in the case of VOICE (see Case 7.5). The choice for a partnering company can vary from a multinational consultant/vendor to a small local company. Ideally, partnering arrangement with overseas companies should lead to a capacity development of local agencies. That is why some governments insist on involving a local partner.

Stronger partnerships have been built around the 'build, operate and transfer' (BOT) or 'build, own, operate and transfer' (BOOT) models.[5] When the private sector operates an e-government application, in some cases it can be reimbursed a fixed fee per transaction, as in Andhra Pradesh (Case 7.10). A revenue sharing model can be used as well.

However, not all public–private partnership projects have been equally successful. As seen by Hanoi and Ho Chi Minh's joint initiative to launch web development projects for business services agencies, a dangerous pitfall is the excessive reliance on outside consultants, which results in lack of real ownership of the project at the government level. The lack of ownership and buy-in cause concern about the feasibility and sustainability of the project without constant help from the private company.[6]

Several governments, as in the case of Mexico, South Africa and a few state governments in India, have been quick to encourage private partnerships as a way to share or transfer start-up costs for e-government projects. While this may be cost effective in the short run, many government agencies find themselves 'locked in' to agreements that offer exclusive privileges to companies in terms of product use and purchase of equipment. Public agencies need to carefully negotiate terms of agreement when entering into private partnerships to avoid giving firms special privileges.

[5] BOT/BOOT (build–own–operate–transfer) is a new concept in infrastructure development that allows direct private sector investment in large-scale projects such as roads, bridges and ICT. To 'build' a private company invests in a public infrastructure project and provides their own financing to construct the project. To 'operate/own', the private company then owns, maintains and manages the facility for an agreed period and gains from the investment through fees. To 'transfer', after the agreed period, the company transfers ownership and operation of the facility to the government.

[6] See full case study at http://www1.worldbank.org/publicsector/egov/vietnam2cities_cs.htm.

For successful execution of public–private partnership strategies, it is important to recognise that the contracting arrangement should deliver gains to all partners. Often the fact that private sector needs to make profits is forgotten by the government contracting agencies. It is a good strategy for governments to implement pilots on their own so that cost structure and implementation issues are well understood. This understanding can be useful in defining contracts when scaled-up versions are being implemented on a wider scale. Implementation of the SmartGov project (Case 7.10) exemplifies how these partnerships can be successfully executed.

5.6 Enabling Legal and Economic Frameworks

A lack of mutual trust between citizens and governments (which is often the case in many developing countries) can be an inhibiting factor in developing e-government. Setting up a legal enabling environment is necessary to build this trust and to validate the use of e-government applications. Creating a certification authority, payment gateways and e-commerce legislation, as well as amending laws to reflect information access, privacy, data security, evidence laws and cyber crimes also need to be considered. In the specialised area of digital signatures, some commentators are of the opinion that written signature requirements pose the greatest stumbling block to the development of electronic commerce and advocate a unified global regulatory scheme for digital signatures. It must be noted that different countries or, in some cases different states within the same country, have considered or proposed digital signature statutes.

Security has several aspects. Transactional security covers electronic communication and contracts, and electronic evidence. Computer network security deals with cyber crime and hackers, as well as viruses. Privacy deals with how data about individuals is collected, processed and disseminated. Data must be fairly and lawfully processed for limited purposes. It should not be kept longer than necessary. It should be processed in accordance with individuals' rights and kept secured. Domestic national security and privacy interests conflict. After 11 September 2001, many governments exempt national security agencies from various privacy law and regulations. Security is also a component for privacy. Thus, use of cryptography for electronic communications is seen as acceptable use of technology to establish privacy. However, such technologies counter the interest of security agencies.

Experience from some developing countries has shown that privacy and security issues do not seem to be deterring issues. Cultural acceptance to government collecting information about an individual is less problematic.

Governments have taken different approaches in implementing a legal framework for e-government and e-commerce. Some have opted for the creation of an umbrella cyber law[7] that encompasses all e-transactions. A large umbrella law saves the need for amending a multitude of laws that address procurement, tax, archives, etc. In some countries waiting for the passing of an umbrella cyber law is too politically contentious, and governments have chosen to amend existing laws to avoid the delays associated with passing a major piece of new legislation.

The UNCITRAL Model Law on Electronic Commerce (hereafter Model Law) is a generic law that can be extended and enhanced by individual countries should they so wish. In devising the Model Law, UNCITRAL had set out to develop rules that could be used in all countries regardless of their technological proficiency or the legal framework under which these countries operated. The Model Law provides generally that electronic communications should be given equivalent legal effect to paper-based communications and specifically addresses how certain types of electronic communications could substitute existing paper-based means of satisfying requirements of writing, signatures and contract formation.[8] The Model Law has been adopted by many countries, including Australia, Hong Kong, the Republic of Korea, Singapore and the Philippines.

Other laws related to the public sector also need to be changed. For example, in Chile the government had to amend the tax code to authorise taxpayers to present their annual reports and accounts, and tax returns online (see Case 7.6). In India legislative changes were needed in implementing registration of property deeds (Case 7.3) and maintaining land records electronically in the case of Bhoomi (Case 7.1).

An enabling economic policy such as liberalisation of the telecom sector that makes the Internet easily accessible can promote widespread use of e-government. In its widest context, privatisation can refer to a

[7] Cyber laws refers to laws regulating the Internet. These can deal from security issues to regulating Intellectual Property Rights over the Internet and rules for dealing with Internet fraud.

[8] Anil Samtani and Harry S.K. Tan, 'Legal, Regulatory and Policy Issues of E-Commerce in Asia', Asian Forum on ICT Policies and Strategies, Kuala Lampur, 18–20 October 2003, http://www.apdip.net/asian-forum/papers/session7.pdf.

range of policies to embrace private sector capital in the development of the industry, everything from outsourcing to full-blown market liberalisation. Privatisation in its narrow sense means full or partial transfer of ownership of a state-owned enterprise to the private sector, usually by share issue privatisation. Overall, the evidence suggests that while privatisation is usually associated with faster fixed-line growth, greater profitability and higher productivity, evidence on prices, net employment effects and capital investment is less clear-cut. One thing most studies agree upon is that the effects of privatisation cannot be easily isolated from the effects of competitive reforms, changes in market structure, and the nature and role of the post-privatisation regulatory regime.

5.7 Incremental Change versus Big Bang

Few management reforms using ICT innovations have the sole aim of reducing corruption or increasing public accountability. Most have both efficiency and other softer goals, and the two goals are intertwined. But stakeholder resistance to corruption and accountability goals is much greater. Corrupt public agencies cannot be expected to embrace such reforms with any enthusiasm. Consequently, a reform strategy to be successful will need to carry out a very thorough and insightful stakeholder analysis and find ways to overcome or bypass the resistance.

Stakeholder analysis will need to distinguish between those likely to benefit, those who will be largely unaffected, those who will suffer minor losses of benefits, privileges, status or power, and those who are likely suffer major losses. The reform strategy will need to address each of these groups. Compromises are generally unavoidable.

The analysis must include both informal reality as well as formal arrangements. Official bureaucracies often have difficulty accepting informal realities that everyone knows exist but few are willing to acknowledge publicly. This will often include major irregularities. In some cases huge amounts of public resources are being diverted to personal benefit, which the reforms, if successful, would stop. For example, posting the tax code on a web site and permitting individual taxpayers to complete self-assessments and submit their tax returns and tax payments electronically will help stop huge private benefits being reaped by tax collectors who previously 'negotiated' with taxpayers. And the same is true for customs officials dealing with importers. Such systems must be backed up with very rigorous spot audits. Control efforts and resources can then focus on preventing corrupt audits. Resistance to such reforms can be vicious. For example, in one instance, customs officers in Bangladesh simply smashed the computers introduced at ports, forcing the reforms to be withdrawn.[9]

In most situations there are individual 'drivers of change' who for various reasons are strongly motivated to support reforms. Generally these are decision makers who are not the beneficiaries of the corruption, who may even resent it, and may see significant political advantage in 'cleaning up' a corrupt agency. Some will be driven by high personal integrity. The reform strategy will need to identify and nurture the drivers of change. These may be both within the public bureaucracy and in civil society—such as citizen watch groups like the national chapters of Transparency International, NGOs both local and international, and the media. In the most difficult cases all such groups will need to be mobilised.

A reform strategy should not be overly ambitious. Incrementalism may triumph over the 'big bang' reform that is sometimes preferred by crusading politicians brought to power on a wave of public revulsion at widespread corruption. In the end what is important is ensuring the sustainability of reform. However, ICT innovations may sometimes bring about system changes that cannot be easily reversed, for example, when accounts and land registries are computerised. These are the reforms to be promoted first. Moreover, some low-level ICT innovations can subtly change the way business is conducted, making it much more transparent, so that the change takes place before those who loose out have realised the consequences and, faced by a fait accompli, find that it is too late to oppose the reform.

5.8 Evaluating E-Government

Many successful applications demonstrate that it is important to identify measurable benefits. Post-implementation audit of benefits, particularly feedback from clients, allows for improvements that add value and expand the client base. To ensure that projects have been evaluated adequately, independent auditing and evaluating has been cited as a best practice.

Currently, there are no frameworks or methodologies to accurately measure the success or failure of an e-government project. Success is often judged on the basis of media reports, recognition by international

---

[9] Pierre Landell-Mills, 'Improving Governance in Bangladesh: The Elements of a New Strategy', http://www.aedsb.org/PLM-BanglaGovernance.htm.

agencies and assessment provided by the project implementers. In all of these cases clients that are supposed to benefit from these projects supply no feedback. If feedback is recorded, it is usually anecdotal and not based on a systematic survey. A recent initiative by the Global Knowledge Sharing Programme of the World Bank in evaluating four successful projects in India through independent agencies has revealed surprising results. Two of the four projects that were recognised as successes are actually showing up as failures.[10] It is important that e-government projects have an in-built component of periodic assessment by an independent agency. This is in addition to a continuing feedback mechanism from the clients.

Practical Methodology for Evaluating E-Government Projects

There are a number of factors that increase the complexity of the evaluation process of e-government applications. E-government applications are characterised by a large number of stakeholders. Often the projects are large and complex, and many of the cost elements are not explicit. For example, change management accounts for nearly 30 to 40 per cent of the effort required in implementing the system and requires significant management attention, the cost of which is difficult to quantify.

Private sector investments are analysed by using the discounted cash flow method that looks for a positive net present value. To compute cash flows one needs to monetise all the benefits and costs. Since many of the benefits of e-government applications are soft, such as more transparency, less corruption and improved service delivery, computing a monetary value is difficult.

Four independent evaluations of projects in India provide a basic methodology to evaluate e-government:

1. Identify all the stakeholders who will be affected by the application. The impact could be positive or negative. For example, the Gujarat checkposts evaluation was conducted through a survey of the stakeholders, which included truck drivers who frequently traverse the Gujarat interstate checkposts, government officials responsible for examining vehicles traversing

---

[10] For complete reports of evaluation of Bhoomi, FRIENDS, Gyandoot and the interstate checkposts in Gujarat, see http://www1.worldbank.org/publicsector/bnpp/egovupdate.htm.

checkposts, trucking companies or transporters that ferrying goods from one location to another for their clients, companies that use the transporters, the solution provider and the private sector company that designed and installed the system. In addition to these stakeholders, a control group of non-users of computerised checkposts from Rajasthan were included in the study (see Case 7.9).

2. Through preliminary discussion with a small sample of different types of stakeholders, the perceived costs and benefits of a system can be assessed. It is useful to draw upon the potential benefits (planned in the project feasibility report) to elicit a meaningful response in the discussions. It is often interesting that some unexpected benefits can be reported in these preliminary discussions. For example, in the case of the FRIENDS project (see Case 7.4) government personnel were extremely happy about their work. The positive perception of civil servants was not a benefit that was anticipated.

3. Develop indicators to measure different types of benefits that have been listed. These could be hard indicators such as bribes paid for a service or soft indicators such as perception of friendliness of operators manning a computerised counter. In the case of bribery, indicators were developed by all four evaluations that surveyed the presence of bribery before and after the e-government application was implemented.

4. Define a sampling plan and procedure for conducting a structured survey to measure different kinds of benefits and costs. The sample size needs to be determined so that the estimates based on the sample can be within an acceptable degree of confidence.

5. Carry out a survey conducted by trained market researchers. The survey agency should be able to work independently of the government or an implementing agency. Bhoomi, for example, was evaluated independently by researchers from Public Affairs Council, Bangalore, thus providing further credibility to Bhoomi's own claims of success.

6. The next step is to analyse the survey data and compile results. The survey data needs to be combined with other data collected from log books and transaction logs. Data on investments and operating costs will have to be collected from the implementing agencies. Finally, the analysis of the benefits and costs has to be presented in a manner so that a judgement regarding the acceptability of the project can be made.

The costs of conducting an evaluation using the above methodology are quite reasonable. In most developing countries it should be possible to evaluate an application with a cost of less than $10,000. Two of the cases in Chapter 7—FRIENDS (Case 7.4) and Bhoomi (Case 7.1)—include the results of such an evaluation. The case on FRIENDS also describes the details of the methodology.

5.9 Understanding Risk Factors in Implementing E-Government Projects

Evaluations of four e-government projects that were deemed to be successful have indicated that at least two projects, Gyandoot (Case 7.2) and the interstate checkposts in Gujarat (Case 7.9) are faltering. An analysis of these projects suggests a number of risk factors that can affect the long-term sustainability of e-government projects.

Often ministerial changes result in a situation where the new minister is not supportive of the ideas and innovations implemented by a predecessor. A similar risk arises because of frequent changes in administrative leadership when key functionaries are transferred. Project initiators need to ensure that key administrative functionaries will have an adequately long tenure to see through the implementation.

Projects that take a very long time to implement are at risk because of rapid changes in technology, and the fact that realisation of benefits comes long after the pains of implementing the application. This tends to heighten resistance. On the other hand, implementation that is hurried through because of political pressure to show quick results, or because of the uncertainty created by short tenures of administrators, carries its own set of risks. Often corners need to be cut and key elements of the application are either not taken up or are done in a shoddy manner.

An inappropriate definition of project scale and scope also results in failure. If the project's scale is ambitions, the task may become unmanageable or resources may run dry. If new and untested technology is used some vital components of an application may not work because of the breakdown of technology. Similarly, a project scope defined too narrowly may not deliver the intended benefits.

It is important to manage expectations of various stakeholders. Often e-government is treated as a panacea for several long-standing ills of a system. It needs to be recognised that governance reform is a multipronged process in which e-government is only one tool among many other changes that need to be made. E-government projects focused on transparency and corruption need to be implemented in a context of wider administrative reform.

Poorly designed systems in terms of underlying architecture, technology and process can lead to implementation failures. If computerisation is partial and not conducted with re-engineering initiatives, many of the benefits do not accrue. Such systems may function for a while because of the higher level of monitoring and supervision, but in the absence of process improvements, such temporary gains cannot be institutionalised.

Considering the degree of change that is involved in implementing e-government projects, there is a temptation to bypass existing employees by outsourcing work to private sector or hiring new recruits. However, unless the resistance among bypassed employees is broken through education, training or any other means, it continues to foster. The system can get sabotaged after the initial champion has left.

Normally close identification of a project with a single powerful champion automatically weakens the support that a project can receive from peers and other departments. It is best not to personalise a project.

5.10 Conclusion

No government is completely ready for e-government, but that does not mean that such projects should not be taken up. It is important to think through a big picture of how e-government will be rolled out over the next four to five years. A balance should be maintained between planning/ co-ordination and action. Experience from many countries has shown that strategy and planning have important roles in creating vision, goals and targets. The articulation of a vision, which could take some time, given the need to reach consensus and win over stakeholders, should not impede the launching of small-scale quick-strike projects. A few quick-strike projects implemented in a nine- to twelve-month time-frame can motivate government agencies to follow suit, and help bring momentum to the conception of a national strategy and legal enabling framework. If there is an overemphasis on planning and coordination (such as forming various committees) and not enough attention is paid to actual implementation, the credibility of the strategy may suffer in the eyes of civil servants.

In devising an e-government strategy there is no one size that fits all. Often very different strategies seem to result in equal success as is illustrated in the case of Andhra Pradesh and Karnataka, the two states that have the maximum number of successful projects in India (see Box 5.2). Chapters 4 and 5 have provided some guiding principles that need to be viewed in the specific social and economic context of a country.

Box 5.2
A Tale of Two States

Karnataka's e-government effort was largely based on several key departmental initiatives. Some of these projects like Bhoomi and Khajane are now up and running, and are beginning to create an impact. In Karnataka there is almost complete reliance on the NIC (a state agency) for development of applications.

Andhra Pradesh (AP) started with a well-articulated vision and strategy in 1999. Two major planks of AP's strategy are: strong partnership with the private sector and a very strong emphasis on capacity development of civil servants. AP's e-government programme is centrally coordinated and many projects are centrally directed. AP also has many successes like CARD and E-Seva. Some projects like SmartGov are technically very sophisticated.

Karnataka has only recently paid attention to the task of developing a vision and strategy for e-government. A strategy paper was formerly launched in October 2002. New institutional arrangements have been created to promote e-governance. A new post of Secretary, E-Governance, has been created in the department of personnel and administrative reform. The task of promoting the growth of the IT sector in Karnataka has been separated from the task of using ICT within the government.

The largest difference is in political support. In Andhra Pradesh the chief minister is very aggressive in pushing the use of technology. Andhra's e-government programme is widely publicised and admired. In Karnataka political support exists but is at a lower key. Karnataka has a few projects that are nationally very visible. In spite of widely different strategies, the outcome at this stage does not appear to be very different because the bulk of the civil service in both states is still keen on preserving the status quo. It is in the long run that AP may benefit because of its investments in capacity building and developing a coherent vision and strategy.

6

The Future of E-Government

Governments around the world are embracing electronic government. In every region of the globe—from developing countries to industrialised ones—national and local governments are putting critical information online, automating once-cumbersome processes and interacting electronically with their citizens. This enthusiasm comes in part from a belief that technology can transform the government's often-negative image. In many places citizens view their governments as bloated, wasteful and unresponsive to their most pressing needs. Mistrust of government is rife among the public and businesses. Civil servants are often seen as profiteers. The spread of information and communication technology (ICT) brings hope that governments can transform. And, indeed, reform-minded officials everywhere are using technology to improve their governments.

But e-government is not a short cut to economic development, budget savings or clean, efficient government. E-government is not the 'Big Bang', a single event that immediately and forever alters the universe of government. E-government is a process, and often a struggle that presents costs and risks, both financial and political. These risks can be significant. If not well conceived and implemented, e-government initiatives can waste resources, fail in their promise to deliver useful services and thus increase public frustration with the government. Particularly in the developing world, where resources are scarce, e-government must target areas with high chances for success and produce 'winners'.

Information and communication technologies have a valuable potential to help meet good governance goals in developing countries.[1] E-government can advance the agenda of governance and fiscal reform, transparency, anti-corruption, empowerment and poverty reduction. However, the

---

[1] R.B. Heeks, 'Understanding E-Governance for Development', i-Government Paper No. 11, IDPM, University of Manchester, http://www.man.ac.uk/idpm_dp.htm.

potential remains largely untapped to date. Good governance is a concept that has recently come into regular use in political science, public administration and, more particularly, development management. It appears alongside such concepts and terms as democracy, civil society, popular participation, human rights, and social and sustainable development.[2] Poor human, organisational and technological infrastructure coupled with inappropriate approaches taken by donors, vendors and governments have resulted into less than optimal exploitation of information and communication technologies.

Good governance can also be conceptualised as a part of a development process; it should be participatory, transparent and accountable in character. Political, social and economic priorities in a country can be framed within the framework of good governance with a broad consensus that the voices of the poorest and most vulnerable will be heard in the decision-making processes regarding allocation of resources. The emergence of the new information and communication technology has all the attributes of imparting added value to the processes that give identity, form and relationships to good governance. However, a word of caution is necessary. E-government should not be seen as a panacea for the complex and well-entrenched problems of corruption and poverty. These problems require multi-pronged action. E-government is one of the many tools whose potential in tackling these problems needs to be recognised. E-government provides an entry point for reform-minded politicians as it is able to make a dent on some of these problems without a head-on confrontation with the vested interests that would like to preserve the status quo. Several successful projects described in this book have shown that gains from e-government can be real, but implementation requires a lot of administrative effort. The challenge is to commit reform-minded politicians to conduct the necessary institutional reforms required for e-government to add value to citizens and businesses. There is no specific sequence in which different kinds of reform are introduced. Often they run a parallel course, depending on the state of the starting condition.

Many of the applications implemented across developing countries may not be seen as true e-government applications as some part of the service delivery, particularly if processing of payments is not electronic.

[2] Rogers W'O Okot-Uma, 'Electronic Governance: Re-inventing Good Governance', Commonwealth Secretariat, London, http://www1.worldbank.org/publicsector/egov/Okot-Uma.pdf.

The delivery model is not self-service and applications that require inter-departmental coordination are still not online. However, the applications have delivered significant benefits to all stakeholders, and that should provide the incentive to go ahead. Earlier chapters and case studies have emphasised implementation challenges and how these can be overcome. Figure 6.1 attempts to capture the critical success factors for different stages of evolution of e-government. Most developing countries fall into the first and second stages. Strong project leadership and coordinated efforts across departments are necessary to evolve to the third and fourth stages. This requires significant institutional reforms in the way government conducts internal businesses and a change in the behaviour of civil servants and managers.

Figure 6.1
Critical Success Factors for Different Stages of E-Government

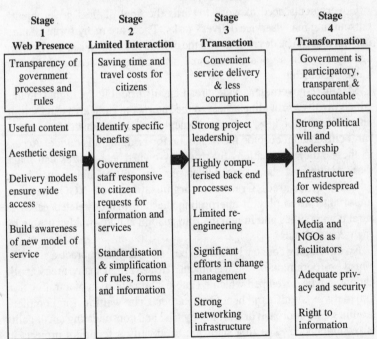

Stage 1 Web Presence	Stage 2 Limited Interaction	Stage 3 Transaction	Stage 4 Transformation
Transparency of government processes and rules	Saving time and travel costs for citizens	Convenient service delivery & less corruption	Government is participatory, transparent & accountable
Useful content Aesthetic design Delivery models ensure wide access Build awareness of new model of service	Identify specific benefits Government staff responsive to citizen requests for information and services Standardisation & simplification of rules, forms and information	Strong project leadership Highly computerised back end processes Limited re-engineering Significant efforts in change management Strong networking infrastructure	Strong political will and leadership Infrastructure for widespread access Media and NGOs as facilitators Adequate privacy and security Right to information

There are diametrically opposite views held about the role of ICT in development. Enthusiasts believe that use of ICT is a necessary condition for development. On the other hand, many development specialists are disillusioned with failed promises.[3] Many cases in this book indicate that ICT use may be necessary but not sufficient to create development. In fact these cases illustrate some of the conditions for sufficiency. In the context of a somewhat poor record of ICT in delivering value commensurate with investments, e-government applications do offer the opportunity to derive significant value for citizens and businesses. A few successful projects have demonstrated how this can be done. There are significant challenges in making e-government widespread. Some of these challenges have been recounted.

E-government projects need to be defined with clearly identified goals and measurable benefits for citizens and businesses. Significant process reform is needed when using ICT for automating procedures for delivering services. Online delivery through assisted community service centres is the most practical solution in countries with low Internet penetration and significant levels of illiteracy.

Governments need to work towards the goal of 'less government', outsourcing many service delivery tasks. There are many forms of partnership that can be developed with the private sector. A quasi-government agency is often a good institutional arrangement to seek and develop these partnerships.

Making e-government widespread entails bridging the digital divide, which involves providing access to the Internet to rural areas and setting up of information kiosks. E-government applications that offer value to rural citizens can become the backbone for bridging this divide. Access to these killer applications by privately-owned tele-centres can make these viable in a short span. Other services will be added once basic viability is ensured. Grassroots organisations and NGOs have an important role to play in interpreting the information-related needs of rural communities and in making information and knowledge usable by such communities.

No developing country is likely to be fully ready to embrace a comprehensive programme of e-government. However, in many areas applications can be developed which e-enable a large portion of a transaction and deliver significant benefits. Rather than waiting for complete readiness, an approach of learning by trial and consolidating small gains is recommended. The first steps are to identify a few pilot projects in

[3] Mayuri Odedra, 'Poor Management Leads to Gross Under-utilisation', *Computers in Africa*, Vol. 4, No. 5, 1990; and Richard Heeks, 'Information Systems and Developing Countries: Failure, Success and Local Improvisations', *Information Society*, Vol. 18, No. 5, 2002, pp. 101–12.

departments that have exposure to computerisation, a large interface with the public and are experiencing problems with corruption. Benefits of implementing the pilots need to be articulated in specific terms. Impact on transparency, corruption and poverty must be the underlying concern. In planning for e-government, countries need to balance their efforts on policy, strategy and action.

A few political leaders and civil servants who believe in the idea of reform have initiated innovative applications. The vast majority, however, is yet to awaken to the potential of e-government for reform. The fundamental problem facing governance reform is that those public officials who need to take corrective actions are the same as those who benefit from governance abuses. Reform will only happen when someone up the management chain has the will and the capacity to impose changes on established systems. The motivation for doing so may be political (the pressure of public opinion) or simply high minded. The former is more dependable. Therefore, those wishing to promote such reforms will need to identify ways to build such positive political pressures.

Political commitment is necessary to initiate the change that is involved. A major task is to build institutional capacity for governance reform. Training packages would have to be developed for senior levels of bureaucracy and political executives on the potential and challenges of implementing e-government. More substantive training programmes will be needed to train chief information officers and project leaders who will implement specific projects. Often e-government is seen to be just technology. Experience from successful projects suggests that technology is just 20 per cent of the whole effort (Figure 6.2). Getting the technology right is important, but process re-engineering and change management demand far greater attention.

Figure 6.2
Enablers of E-Government

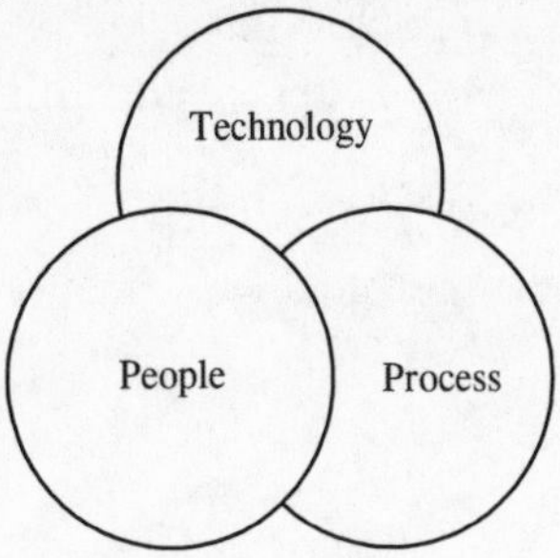

- 20% technology
- 30% business process re-engineering
- 40% change management
- 10% managing partners

A large number of sceptics still need to be convinced that investments in ICT are as essential as in other forms of infrastructure. Perhaps more projects and documented research on the impact created by e-government initiatives and the factors that enable successful implementation can provide the clinching argument. This book is an attempt to fulfil this need.

7

Case Studies of Social and Economic Impacts of E-Government

Documented research on the social or economic impact of e-government initiatives is virtually non-existent. Currently available information is largely anecdotal. It is worth noting that documented case studies often highlight success stories. There may be a significant number of failed projects which do not find a mention in this book. This chapter includes twelve case studies of e-government applications that illustrate services to different types of clients and a variety of benefits. Every case has shades of successes and some elements that have not worked so well. There is learning to be derived from both successes and failures. The cases are structured to present the problems with earlier manual methods, the details of the new approach, implementation challenges that were faced, costs and benefit delivered, and key lessons that can be learnt by others who wish to implement e-government systems. Case studies 7.1 to 7.5 have been chosen because they have demonstrated some impact on poverty alleviation, empowerment of citizens, and increased transparency and lowered corruption in service delivery. Cases 7.6 to 7.11 have been chosen because they illustrated some impact on revenue collections by the government, improving service delivery to businesses, improving transparency and reducing costs in government procurement, and reducing corruption in service delivery to businesses. The last case is significantly different from all the other cases as it does not focus on service delivery and has no transactional elements. It demonstrates the potential impact of web publishing on transparency and corruption in society. All the cases exemplify many of the critical success factors discussed in Chapters 3 and 4. Table 7.1 provides a brief description of the application covered in each case.

Table 7.1
Cases Included in the Chapter

Title of the case	Brief description
Bhoomi: Computerisation of Land Records	A printed copy of the RTC (a land title document needed for many tasks such as obtaining bank loans) can be obtained online in 15 minutes at any of the 177 computerised kiosks in Karnataka, India, on payment of a small fee.
Gyandoot: Community-Owned Rural Internet Kiosks	Rural citizens have the opportunity to access knowledge and a number of government services on payment of a small service fee. Thirty-nine privately owned kiosks connect with a district administration server through an intranet. The project is faltering after initial success.
CARD: Computer-Aided Registration of Deeds	Property deeds can be registered at 240 offices in a couple of hours instead of several days as in the manual system.
FRIENDS: Online Payments to the Government in Kerala	Utility bills and other payments to various government departments can be made online at service centres at district headquarters.
VOICE: Computerised Service Centres for Municipal Services	The VOICE system publishes information relating to municipal government services, permits and licences. It enables citizens to track the progress of their applications, thus making the entire system transparent.
Online Income Tax Administration	An interactive web site that contains basic information pertaining to tax laws and procedures, and permits tax-payers to file annual declarations and make tax payments electronically.
E-procurement: Experiences from the Developing World	These web-based procurement systems permit registration of vendors, display of request for bids by government departments, electronic bid submission by the vendors, reverse auctions and publication of results after suppliers are selected.
Indian Customs Online	Import/export documentation is now processed electronically through a workflow software. Cargo handling agents can file the documents from their own computers.
Computerised Interstate Checkposts in Gujarat	Use of computers/electronic devices at ten remote interstate border checkposts in Gujarat, India, collect fines from overloaded trucks. It has significantly increased the state's revenue, but has had a marginal impact on corruption.

(Table 7.1 contd.)

Title of the case	Brief description
SmartGov: Andhra Pradesh Sachivalaya E-Application	This has introduced a paper-less environment in the state Secretariat using workflow software. It has resulted in increased efficiency and transparency.
OPEN: Seoul's Anti-Corruption Project	The system exemplifies the impact on corruption of making transparent the decision-making processes and actions of individual civil servants. It publishes information and enables tracking of individual application for permits and licences issued by the local government.
Central Vigilance Commission Web Site: A Bold Anti-Corruption Experiment	To propagate the idea of zero tolerance for corruption, this web site publishes information such as the names of senior officers against whom investigations have been ordered or penalties imposed for corruption, performance of investigating agencies and procedure for filing complaints.

Most of these cases were initially documented in 2000–2001, about a year after the application had been implemented. They were updated in 2003 at the time of writing this book to incorporate recent data and information available from formal and informal evaluations. The purpose of including these cases is not to pronounce them as successes or failures. In fact, the degree of perceived success may change as time progresses, project implementers make way for new teams, and political support weakens or strengthens. These cases do not merely present facts at a point of time, but include analysis of the process of developing these applications to provide learning for those who will strategise and implement e-government in different contexts in the future. The cases are not intended to serve as best practice examples that can be replicated in other contexts. Readers are encouraged to seek more details in case a similar application is to be implemented in another context.

Case 7.1: Bhoomi—Computerisation of Land Records

The Department of Revenue in Karnataka, India has computerised 20 million records of land ownership of 6.7 million farmers in the state. Previously, farmers had to seek out the village accountant to get a copy of the Record of Rights, Tenancy and Crops (RTC), a document needed for many tasks such as obtaining bank loans. There were delays and harassment; bribes had to be paid. Today, for a fee of Rs 15, a printed copy of the RTC can be obtained online at computerised land record kiosks (Bhoomi centres) in 177 taluk offices. In the next phase all the taluk databases are to be uploaded to a web-enabled central database. RTCs would then be available online at Internet kiosks, which are likely to be set up in rural areas.

Application Context

In the manual system, land records were maintained by 9,000 village accountants, each serving a cluster of three to four villages. Two types of records were maintained: (*a*) registers, which indicated the current ownership of each parcel of land, its area and cropping pattern; and (*b*) village maps that reflected the boundaries of each parcel. Requests to alter land records (upon sale or inheritance of a land parcel) had to be filed with the village accountant. However, for various reasons, the village accountant could afford to ignore these 'mutation' requests. Upon receiving a request, the village accountant is required to issue notices to the interested parties and also paste the notice at the village office. Often neither of these actions was carried out, and no record of the notices was maintained. Notices were rarely sent through post.

An updation of the land records was to be carried out by a revenue inspector if no objections were received within a thirty-day period. In practice, however, it could take up to years for the records to be updated.

Landowners find it difficult to access the village accountant as his duties entail travelling. The time taken by him to provide RTCs has ranged from three to thirty days, depending upon the importance of the record for the farmer and the size of the bribe. A typical bribe for a certificate could range from Rs 100 to Rs 2,000. If some details were to be written in an ambiguous fashion, out of selfish motives, the bribe could go up to Rs 10,000. Land records in the custody of village accountant were not open to public scrutiny.

Over time several inaccuracies crept into the old system through improper manipulation by the village accountant, particularly with respect to government land. Even where accountants were law-abiding, village maps could not remain accurate as land was parcelled into very small lots over generations. The system of physical verification of records by deputy *tehsildars* (supervisors of village accountants) became weak as the number of records multiplied and these functionaries were burdened with a host of other regulatory and developmental work.

The central and state governments had long been aware of the need to reform the land record system. The beginning of computerisation of land records in Karnataka goes back to 1991 when the first pilot was initiated through a centrally sponsored scheme, fully funded by the Government of India. By 1996 projects for computerisation of land records were sanctioned for all districts in the state of Karnataka. However, no provision was made to install computers at the *taluk* level where manual records were actually updated. The project fizzled out without achieving its objective of creating a clean, up-to-date database.

A New Approach

Today, a computerised land record kiosk (Bhoomi centre) is operational in all the 177 *taluk*s in Karnataka. At these *taluk* offices a farmer can obtain a copy of an RTC online by paying a Rs 15 fee. A second computer screen faces the clients to enable them to see the transaction being performed. Copies can be obtained for any land parcel in the *taluk* by providing the name of the owner or the plot number. A village accountant is available full-time at these kiosks.

When a change of ownership takes place through sale or inheritance, farmers can file for a mutation of the land record at the Bhoomi centre. Each request is assigned a number by the computer. The number can be used to check the status of the application on a touch screen provided on a pilot basis in three of the computerised kiosks. The computer automatically generates notices, which are then handed over to the village accountant stationed in the field who is responsible for servicing the particular village. Most village accountants stationed in the field visit the central *taluk* office once in two to three days to pick these papers.

The process of issuing notices by village accountants to the interested parties remains the same. And as before, the revenue inspector who is stationed in the field approves changes to the land record thirty days after the notices are served, provided that there are no objections. A significant change in the process makes it mandatory to stick to a first-come-first-serve discipline. It takes a few days for the approval to reach the Bhoomi kiosk, where it is scanned on the day of its arrival. An inward and outward register is maintained. The updated RTC is printed at the Bhoomi kiosk and handed over to the village accountant for her record. The new owner receives a copy on demand. Bhoomi kiosks create scanned copies of the original mutation orders and notices to avoid unnecessary litigation due to claims that the notices were not served.

With the computerised system, administrators can quickly determine the number of approved and overdue mutation orders. Information collected from one urban *taluk* indicates that 3,000 mutations were handled annually earlier. After computerisation, there has been a 50 per cent jump in the number of mutation requests. This change seems to indicate a level of approval of the new system by the citizens, and willingness to update changes in landownership that were previously left undocumented.

The Bhoomi software incorporates the bio-logon metrics system from Compaq, which authenticates all users of the software using their fingerprint. A log is maintained of all transactions in a session. This makes an officer accountable for her decisions and actions. The government also has plans to web-enable the database to make available to the farmer a copy of the land record locally through an Internet kiosk—although without a signature such a copy will only have an informative value.

A government order decentralising Bhoomi to the village level has been passed. There are plans for opening 1,000 kiosks state-wide, with public–private partnerships. In a pilot experiment, twenty tele-centres have been established in Mandya district by N-Logue[1] using the corDECT technology developed by the Indian Institute of Technology, Madras. These private kiosks can connect to the Mandya database through the N-Logue network and view, print and distribute the land records. The Internet printing model became functional in October 2003. These tele-centres will charge a fee of Rs 25 instead of Rs 15, enabling them to retain Rs 10 per RTC to cover their operational costs and provide a small return on the investment. Most of the users spend Rs 25 to 50 in travelling to a *taluk* kiosk. Some of the users, when questioned about the additional fee, indicated that an additional charge of Rs 10 would be totally acceptable to the farmer community if the RTC could be delivered through a rural tele-centre.

Other services, such as download of 100 important forms for services and beneficiary-oriented schemes, could be added to the content. Departments such as forestry, animal husbandry, sericulture and cottage industries could create content in their own domains for delivery to rural areas. A fee of Rs 10 per RTC collected by the owner will make 1,000 rural kiosks viable in rural Karnataka. User fee being collected by Bhoomi

---

[1] N-Logue Communications Pvt. Ltd is a private company promoted by the Telecommunications and Computer Networking Group of the Indian Institute of Technology, Madras.

is approximately Rs 100 million annually. If 50 per cent of the RTCs are issued from 1,000 rural kiosks that are proposed to be set up, each kiosk will earn an average annual revenue of Rs 50,000. Accounting for variability across kiosks, the floor earning could be in the range of Rs 30,000. At this level of earning a kiosk can be viable.

In another pilot, around 200 village accountants have been given Simputers (locally developed handheld computers) costing about Rs 3.5 million. One round of crop updating for 600 villages was done using Simputers. The second round of crop updating was done in the last quarter of 2003. Teething problems such as maintenance and software bugs have been manageable. However, a further expansion has to wait until the cost of such handheld devices reduces appreciably.

Implementation Challenges

Roll-out of the application to 177 locations was a challenge due to the poor quality of manual records and the enormity of the data entry task. In the first phase the project was implemented on a pilot basis in a controlled environment at four *taluk*s. After gaining experience in data entry operations and implementation of the software, the scheme was extended to one pilot *taluk* in each of the twenty-seven districts. In the third phase the project was rolled out simultaneously to all the remaining 177 *taluk*s.

Records in the field were not up-to-date due to poor work culture and lack of training amongst the revenue staff. Also, farmers often do not report transactions within the family either because they are discouraged by the attitude of the revenue staff or due to internal family problems. The maintenance of land records is not uniform across districts.

As revenue officials were not interested in data entry, private data entry agencies tackled the 20,000 man-months of work in an offline mode at the *taluk* level. A comprehensive software that accommodated all variations in manual records across districts was used. After the initial data entry, prints were validated against the original record books by the village accountants.

Many problems were encountered in offline data entry. The process was slow and error prone due to poor work quality by data entry agencies. Technical guidance from officers of the district informatics centre was not easily available as they were overloaded with other work. And data entry agencies were unwilling to recruit more manpower as it required investment in training on a specialised data entry software, which would not be useful to them for other projects. Moreover, interruptions in electrical power in the *taluk* headquarters and delay in maintenance of computers at the *taluk* level by vendors were a problem.

Every district has been provided with a consultant to act as a bridge between the data entry agency and the district administration. After the system is operational, the consultant trains the *taluk* staff and helps the district administration in day-to-day work at the Bhoomi kiosk.

Operators have been provided for one year to handle online data entry at the Bhoomi kiosks. Village accountants will take over the work of these operators after a year. A comprehensive training module was designed jointly by the department and the National Informatics Centre (NIC, a software development agency of the central government) to train the accountants. Training lasted for seven days, 11 hours each day, followed by a paper-less test on the last day.

The village accountants who would be in charge of the new kiosks were chosen very carefully. Young persons fresh out of college were recruited and trained at the headquarters. These officials had not experienced the power that a village accountant could exercise over rural farmers. The project leader (additional secretary of the department) personally participated in the training given to every batch of accountants to ensure that they felt complete ownership and a sense of importance in being assigned to this new initiative. Accountants were encouraged to talk to the project leader either at his home or at his office. Nearly 500 officials, including all deputy *tahsildar*s, were trained at the state headquarters and more than 1,000 officials were trained by the Bhoomi consultants at the district level.

Challenge of Getting the Staff on Board

To allay the fears of field officials that their job descriptions would change in a major way, twelve state-level information seminars were organised for 1,200 senior and mid-level officers. Additionally, four division-level workshops were organised to train 800 officials. These seminars emphasised that maintenance of land records was only one of their many functions and that computerisation would remove the drudgery of maintaining these records manually. Revenue officials would continue to be responsible for field enquiry. Reducing corruption was not a key message at these gatherings.

The political executive was completely involved in the computerisation project. The state chief minister and revenue minister highlighted the importance of the project publicly. The chief minister wrote regularly to all district deputy commissioners, exhorting them to get fully involved in the computerisation. He inaugurated a large number of land record kiosks. Meanwhile, the revenue minister regularly reviewed the computerisation process and also inaugurated a large number of kiosks. A committee of Members of the Legislative Assembly (MLAs) visited the kiosks and deputy commissioners invited MLAs of their districts to witness the functioning of kiosks. All this helped demonstrate that there was a strong political will for computerisation.

Selected field-level personnel were invited to participate in the software development process for various Bhoomi modules through a formal state-level Bhoomi committee. Meetings were held with participation from various levels in the department to elicit suggestions for improvement; and decisions taken at these meetings were incorporated into the software design. Nearly 125 person-months were spent on software development. A further effort of thirty person-months will be needed to upgrade to the next version.

Field supervision is critical to roll-out any new system. The project leader in charge preferred to appoint four independent consultants who could tour sites randomly in each division and report on the problems and progress of Bhoomi. Appointing consultants turned out to be problematic, as the central government project did not permit such a line item of expenditure. The expected cost was Rs 1.5 million.

Evaluation of Bhoomi

Improving the land record delivery system has a significant social and economic impact in rural areas. Nearly 2,500 bank branches in Karnataka loan approximately Rs 40 billion to farmers as working capital every year. A copy of the RTC is absolutely essential for the farmer to procure the loan. Effective land record management can help banks in recovery. More than 70 per cent disputes in courts are land based. Adjudication of disputes can be faster if access to land records is made efficient. Bhoomi as a transparent land record system is a vast improvement over the manual system that it has replaced.

For a fee of Rs 15, a printed copy of the RTC could be obtained online in minutes at computerised Bhoomi kiosks in 177 *taluk* offices. The land records are in the public domain. Copies of RTC can be obtained for any land parcel in the *taluk* by providing the name of the owner or the plot (survey) number. Any record can be viewed through a touch screen at a few kiosks.

Farmers can apply for mutation and expedite the process by reviewing the status of their request online, presenting documentary evidence to supervisors in the event that their request is not processed within the stipulated time period. With the computerised system, administrators can quickly determine the number of approved and overdue mutation orders. Information collected from one urban *taluk* indicates that earlier 3,000 mutations were handled annually. After computerisation, there has been a 50 per cent jump. This change would seem to indicate a level of approval of the new system by the citizens, and willingness to update changes in landownership that were previously left undocumented.

By the end of May 2002 the annual revenue generated through issuance of RTCs was Rs 40 million, and the monthly collection had stabilised to about Rs 7 million. It is estimated that between Rs 90 and 100 million will be collected each year from charges for RTCs. Nearly 78.3 per cent of all Bhoomi users take an RTC whereas 17.2 per cent apply for a modified RTC (involving mutation) and 4.5 per cent collect a copy of the mutation order. The users of Bhoomi collect these documents for a variety of reasons. The largest proportion of users (51 per cent) collect the RTCs for applying for loan from a bank. Nearly 14 per cent use an RTC to verify the outcome of a mutation request. About 16 per cent use the documents in courts or to verify details of adjoining property.

Bhoomi is one of the few e-government applications that have been evaluated by an independent agency. An evaluation conducted by the Public Affairs Centre, Bangalore, in July 2002 showed significant impact on efficiency in delivery and corruption[2]:

---

[2] The report card on the Bhoomi initiative sought to assess benefits derived by users of Bhoomi centres in relation to improved quality of service and satisfaction. A sample survey was carried out among citizens who have used Bhoomi kiosks as well as a control sample of those who have used non-computerised land record providers. Quality of service and user satisfaction was compared across these two groups to derive conclusions on the impact and benefit from the Bhoomi initiative. Data was collected from six districts reflecting geographic regions of Karnataka, and two Bhoomi kiosks were selected through sampling (weighted by intensity of use) among the kiosks operating in each district. A total of 198 respondents were interviewed across the Bhoomi kiosks. For the non-computerised facility user sample, four *taluks* were selected and fifty-nine respondents interviewed. A team from A.C. Nielsen and ORG-MARG carried out the field survey and preliminary analysis. (Source: Public Affairs Centre, Bangalore, 2002, http://www1.worldbank.org/publicsector/egov/cvc_cs.htm.)

1. **Ease in use of the Bhoomi kiosks:** Many users (66 per cent) were able to utilise the Bhoomi kiosks with no help, in contrast with 25 per cent in the case of the manual system. Most users of the Bhoomi system (78 per cent) found the system to be very simple. Many Bhoomi users (68 per cent) had also made use of the manual system in the past; a majority of users (78 per cent) who had past experience with the manual system found the Bhoomi system more simple.

2. **Complexity of procedures:** Most users (79 per cent) of Bhoomi kiosks did so without having to meet any official except the counter staff. In contrast, in the earlier manual system, users had to meet a minimum of one official (19 per cent). The extent of complexity is reflected in the fact that 61 per cent users of the manual system had to meet two to four officials for their work. Legacies of the manual system have not completely faded away. About 18 per cent of Bhoomi users reported that their document was not signed by the appointed village accountant operating the kiosk, 6 per cent reported that they filled out an application form for the issue of an RTC.

3. **Errors in documents received:** Users indicated that the Bhoomi kiosks provided error-free documents to more users (74 per cent), in contrast with 63 per cent in the case of the manual system. Among those reporting errors, wrongly spelt names were the most frequent (81 per cent in case of manual system and 53 per cent in the Bhoomi system). However, major errors in land details were noticed by 31 per cent of those who reported errors in the manual system, in contrast with 4 per cent in case of Bhoomi users.

4. **Rectifying errors:** Given that errors are not unusual at this stage of development of the Bhoomi system, how efficient are the response systems? Almost all users of the Bhoomi system had confidence to complain and sought rectification (93 per cent) as compared to less than half (49 per cent) in the manual system. Half the complainants (58 per cent) got timely response in case of Bhoomi, while such response was reported by only 4 per cent of those using the manual system.

5. **Cost of service:** All users of the Bhoomi facility who wish to receive a hard copy of the RTC are to pay a fee of Rs 15 each and receive a receipt for the same. A large segment of users

(66 per cent) reported that they did not get a receipt for the payment they made.

6. **Hidden costs:** Citizens also incur hidden costs of time and effort to secure these certificates. Most Bhoomi users (79 per cent) reported a minimal waiting time in the queue of 10 minutes or less, in contrast with 27 per cent who could meet the concerned official in such short time. The bigger issue is the number of times a citizen had to visit these offices to get the certificate. While most users got the RTC (72 per cent) one visit to the Bhoomi kiosk, only 5 per cent got it that fast in the manual system.

7. **Reduced corruption:** The most serious issue is that of corruption and bribery. Two-thirds of the users of the manual system paid a bribe and 66 per cent of them reported having to do so very often. In contrast, only 3 per cent of the users of the Bhoomi system reported paying bribes.

8. **Staff behaviour:** While the technical capacity of the system plays an important role in its success, the approach of people who handle these task is of critical significance, too. Most Bhoomi users (85 per cent) rated staff behaviour at the Bhoomi kiosks as 'good'; none of the users of the manual system rated staff behaviour as 'good'.

Bhoomi empowers the small rural farmer in many ways. Their relationship with lower rungs of civil servants can be on a more equal footing. Armed with genuine certificates, farmers can raise loans for a variety of purposes and cannot be easily harassed by bank staff. Mutations became an instrument for rural corruption, exploitation and oppression. In case of disputes, landowners simply bribed the officials to get the records changed to favour their position. Now the records are in the public domain and can be easily verified by anyone.

Benefits and Costs

The expenditure on data entry operations for about 2 million RTCs in twenty-seven districts was Rs 80 million. The unit cost of providing hardware and construction of computer rooms and kiosks was of the order of Rs 0.64 million for each *taluk*. Thus, the total out-of-pocket expenditure on the project was Rs 185 million. This does not include the cost of software development done gratis by the NIC.

The cost of processing an RTC has been roughly estimated at Rs 13, assuming a life of five years for the hardware and an activity level of 2 million RTCs issued from all the kiosks (10 per cent of all holdings). This cost includes an assumed operational expenditure of Rs 2 for stationery, cartridges and electricity. The current user fee of Rs 15 seems sufficient to cover these costs. However, if the scheme is extended to 700 sub-*taluk* offices, then there would be an additional expenditure of Rs 0.25 million per kiosk on hardware (1 PC-Rs 45,000; printer-Rs 20,000; UPS-Rs 5,000; generator-Rs 30,000) and site preparation, raising the unit cost of processing above Rs 15 per record.

By the end of November 2001, Rs 5 million had been collected through user fees for the distribution of 330,000 RTCs through 140 kiosks operational for periods varying from three to twelve months. An additional 12,000 RTCs were issued for official purposes.

The benefit in terms of person-days saved is approximately 1.32 million per annum, leading to savings of Rs 66 million per annum in wages. The weighted average value of bribe paid in the manual system was Rs 152.46 per person, while that in Bhoomi was Rs 3.09. Even if we reduce the saving by the fee that they have to pay, of Rs 15, the net saving is Rs 134.37, and translates to a saving of over Rs 806 million annually.

Potential Future Benefits

There are plans to use the Bhoomi kiosk for disseminating other information, like lists of destitute and handicapped pensioners, families living below the poverty line, concessional food grain card holders, *mandi* rates and weather information. Such information is already available at one *taluk* on a pilot basis.

The system generates various types of reports on landownership by size, type of soil, crops, owner's sex, etc., which would be useful for planning poverty alleviation programmes and supplying agricultural inputs. Banks and other lending institutions could be provided electronic access to the database for processing requests for crop loans, and conduct some advance planning on the quantum of lending required. Similarly, the high court, district and *taluk* courts could access the database for resolving legal disputes surrounding land. The system could also lead to better administration of the Land Reforms Act, such as enforcing a ceiling on landholdings.

Key Lessons

Implementation of land records computerisation has been difficult in India. Bhoomi succeeded because there was a champion who worked a 15-hour day for over a year, devoting 80 per cent of his time to the project. Minimising resistance from staff by harnessing political support was an important contributory factor. Extensive training coupled with a participatory style also helped to diminish resistance.

Project managers need to balance the potential benefits against the risk of implementation failure in deciding how much reform (re-engineering) to tackle at any one time. In Bhoomi, significant benefits are delivered in issuing RTCs, but much of the old mutation process remains unaltered. As there is no change in the role of the revenue inspector in passing the mutation order, corruption in the mutation process has not necessarily reduced. Bhoomi has reduced the discretion of public officials by introducing provisions for recording a mutation request online. Farmers can now access the database and are empowered to follow up. Reports on overdue mutations can point to errant behaviour. Still, supervisors must examine the reports and take appropriate action. In remote areas operators can turn away citizens by telling that the system offering online service is down. Strict field supervision is needed (through empowered citizens committees and NGOs) to curb such behaviour. Ultimately, the only recourse that a citizen has against such practices is to lodge a complaint. The process for lodging a complaint should be facilitated through the web. The back end has to be geared to handle complaints received electronically.

As an implementation strategy, manually written RTCs were declared illegal from the day on which the computerised system became operational in a *taluk*. The notification was issued on a *taluk*-by-*taluk* basis as and when the scheme became operational there. This forced the department and the farmers to completely rely on the new system. The strategy worked because the application design was robust and did not falter.

There was some concern in Karnataka about raising the user fee to Rs 15 from Rs 2 in the manual system. Often these fears about user fees are exaggerated, particularly if services have genuinely been improved. The response of the people at *taluk* level has been overwhelming. Queues can be seen at the kiosks in 140 *taluk* centres, and 330,000 people have paid the fee without grumbling.

Soon after the initial success, elected representatives, district officials and farmers made demands that Bhoomi be extended to the sub-*taluk* level. Presumably, the project was considered an unqualified success. However, this expansion would have increased the costs without necessarily increasing the number of RTCs that would have been issued. The department did well to resist the temptation as it would not have been able to monitor and support a geographically spread out operation. In any case, systems should be allowed to stabilise and prove their sustainability over a two-year period before attempting any replication. Many years ago, a District Rural Development Agency computerisation project called CRISP was replicated in 500 districts in a hurried manner. The expansion turned out to be a failure.

The department did well to explore other possibilities, short of direct expansion, that could make RTCs available at sub-*taluk* level. Plans to allow private rural kiosks to issue unsigned copies may never have come about if a hurried expansion of the Bhoomi system had been made. If such copies can be accepted by banks and verified by accessing the departmental database, the need for signed copies will be reduced. A solution may emerge through wider consultations with the ultimate consumers of these documents.

Sources

Rajeev Chawla and Subhash Bhatnagar, 'Bhoomi: Online Delivery of Land Titles in Karnataka, India', Case Study, World Bank, 2002, http://www1.worldbank.org/publicsector/egov/bhoomi_cs.htm.

S.C. Bhatnagar, 'BHOOMI: Closing the Digital Divide through Innovative Reforms and Partnership', Eleventh International Anti-Corruption Conference, Seoul, Republic of Korea, 25–28 May 2003, http://www.11iacc.org/download/0618/WS_11.3_Bhatnagar_Final_Paper.doc.

Albert Lobo and Suresh Balakrishnan, 'Report Card on Service of Bhoomi Kiosks: An Assessment of Benefits by Users of the Computerised Land Records System in Karnataka', Public Affairs Centre, Bangalore, November 2002, http://www1.worldbank.org/publicsector/bnpp/Bhoomi.pdf.

K.M. Baharul Islam 'Information Age Government: Success Stories of Online Land Records & Revenue Governance from India', Executive Summary, Third Meeting of the Committee on Development Information (CODI), Economic Commission for Africa, United Nations Economic and Social Council, Ethiopia, 10–17 May 2003, http://www.uneca.org/codi/Documents/PDF/Information%20Age%20Government.pdf.

Vivek Gupta, 'E-Governance: Lessons from District Computerization', *IFIP Newsletter*, Vol. 12, No. 1, 2002.

'CLR Delivers Grassroots E-Governance', http://www.expresscomputeronline.com/20030324/focus3.shtml.

Case 7.2: Gyandoot—Community-Owned Rural Internet Kiosks

In awarding the Gyandoot project the Stockholm Challenge IT Award 2000 in the Public Service and Democracy category, the jury described it as 'a unique government-to-citizen intranet project . . . with numerous benefits to the region, including a people-based self-reliant sustainable strategy. Gyandoot is recognised as a breakthrough in e-government, demonstrating a paradigm shift which gives marginalised tribal citizens their first ever chance to access knowledge, with minimum investment.' The project also was awarded the CSI-TCS National Award for Best IT Usage for the year 2000. Subsequent evaluations carried out in 2002–3 indicate that the project has begun to falter.

Application Context

Dhar district in central India has a population of 1.7 million; 60 per cent live below the poverty line. The goal of the Gyandoot project was to establish community-owned, technologically innovative and sustainable information kiosks in a poverty-stricken, tribal-dominated rural area of Madhya Pradesh. During the design phase of the project, meetings were held with villagers to gather their input. Among the concerns highlighted by villagers was the absence of information about prevailing agriculture produce auction centre rates. Consequently, farmers were unable to get the best price for their agricultural produce. Copies of land records also were difficult to obtain. A villager had to go out in search of the *patwari* (village functionary who maintains all land records), who was often difficult to get hold of as his duties include extensive travel. To file complaints or submit applications, people had to go to the district headquarters (which could be over 150 km away), resulting in a loss of wages/earnings.

A New Approach

The Gyandoot project was launched on 1 January 2000, with the installation of a low-cost rural intranet covering twenty village information kiosks in five blocks of the district. Later eleven more kiosks were set up. Villages that function as block headquarters or hold weekly markets in tribal areas or are located on major roads were chosen for establishing these kiosks. Seven centres were located in towns (urban areas), eight in large villages with a population of 5,000 to 6,000, another seven in medium-sized villages with a population of 1,000 to 4,000, and the rest in small villages with population of less than 500. Each kiosk caters to about twenty-five to thirty villages. The entire network of thirty-one kiosks covers 311 panchayats (village committees), over 600 villages and a population of around half a million (nearly 50 per cent of the entire district).

Kiosks have been established in the village panchayat buildings. Information kiosks have dial-up connectivity through local exchanges on optical fibre or UHF links. The hub is a remote access server housed in the computer room in the district panchayat.

User fees are charged at the kiosks for the services provided. Local rural youth act as entrepreneurs, running these information kiosks along commercial lines. At the inception of the project it was decided that further expansion of kiosk centres would take place only when local youth come forward to start new centres as private enterprises.

A local person with a ten-year schooling (matriculate) can be selected as an operator. He/she needs only maintenance, limited typing (software is menu driven) and numeric data entry skills. For the initial kiosks, village committees each selected three candidates to receive training at the district council. At the end of the training the best trainees were selected to run a kiosk.

The following services are offered at the kiosks:

1. **Agriculture produce auction centres rates:** Prevailing rates of prominent crops at the local and other recognised auction centres around the country are available online for a nominal charge of Rs 5. The volume of incoming agricultural produce, previous rates, etc., are also provided on demand.
2. **Copies of land records:** Documents relating to land records, including *khasra* (record of rights), are provided on the spot at a charge of Rs 15. All banks in the district have agreed to accept these kiosk documents. Approximately 0.2 million farmers require these extracts at every cropping season to obtain loans from banks for purchasing seeds and fertilisers.
3. **Online registration of applications:** Villagers had to make several visits to the local revenue court to file applications for obtaining income/caste/domicile certificates. Now they may send the application from a kiosk at a cost of only Rs 10. Within ten

days notification about the readiness of the certificate is sent via e-mail to the relevant kiosk. Only one trip is needed—to collect the certificate.

4. **Online public grievance redressal:** A complaint can be filed and a reply received within seven days for a cost of Rs 10. These can include complaints regarding drinking water, quality of seed/ fertiliser, scholarship sanction/disbursement, employee establishment matters, functioning of schools or village committees, etc.

5. **Village auction site:** This facility began in July 2000. It makes auction facilities available to farmers and villagers for land, agricultural machinery, equipment and other durable commodities. One can put one's commodity on sale for a charge of Rs 25 for three months. The list of saleable commodities can be browsed for Rs 10.

6. **Transparency in government:** Updated information regarding beneficiaries of social security pension, beneficiaries of rural development schemes, information regarding government grants given to village committees, public distributions, data on families below the poverty line, etc., are all available on the intranet, which makes government functioning more transparent.

Other services offered at the kiosks include online matrimonial advertisements, information regarding government programmes, a forum for school children to ask questions and talk to an expert and e-mail (free for information on child labour, child marriage, illegal possession of land belonging to Scheduled Tribes, etc.). Some kiosks also have added photocopy machines, STD, PCO and horoscope services. In January 2000, the first month of operation, the kiosk network was accessed 1,200 times for a variety of services. That number reached nearly 9,000 in July. During the first eleven months, the thirty-one Gyandoot kiosks were used nearly 55,000 times.

Twice each day, the person managing the server prints the complaints, applications and e-mails received and sends them to the appropriate authority. The collector responds to certain queries and complaints. If a complaint cannot be addressed, a reply is forwarded to the kiosk manager. The action necessary to address the problem in the field is expected to be taken in seven to ten days. A reply is received at the server room, which is forwarded to the kiosk manager. The district is in the process of putting up a local area network (LAN) connecting major departments (health, education, tribal development, revenue, food, agriculture, public health engineering, district council and district magistrate) to the Gyandoot server. This will eliminate the manual handling of papers.

Implementation Challenges

In the initial phase there were reliability problems with the dial-up connection. Most of the local rural telephone exchanges (LRTE) did not operate with optical fibre cables. Now the telecommunications department has upgraded the connections of all LRTEs to which Gyandoot kiosks are connected. Poor or no connectivity reduces the economic viability of the kiosk and decreases the motivation level of the kiosk manager to be a partner in the project. Telephones have not reached many parts of the hinterland, and expansion of the project to these locales may require other technologies such as wireless.

Senior politicians have been convinced of the merits of the Gyandoot project through demonstration of the facilities provided. The Member of Parliament (MP) from the district allocated 25 per cent of the developmental funds (Rs 20 million) at his disposal for an e-education project in the district. However, small-time politicians and the lower-level bureaucracy have attempted to scuttle the programme as they perceive a loss of power when the delivery system bypasses them. The success of the project depends on the motivation of the kiosk manager, which has been maintained at a high level through regular contact/training.

Although complaint filing has been structured through a menu, numerous complaints are sent using the e-mail facility in local languages, which make them difficult or impossible to address. To enhance the economic viability of kiosks, they are being given licences to vend government judicial stamps and delegated powers to write petitions. In addition, a public awareness campaign has been launched in the district to promote the kiosks. From the funds available with Gyandoot, two scholarships of Rs 1,000 each will be awarded each month for five years. Only those students of the district who motivate ten or more villagers to use Gyandoot facilities during a specified time window will be eligible. School students of senior classes are being taken to the nearest kiosk on study tours. Gyandoot Computer Clubs are being established in major high schools and higher secondary schools of the district. Special *gram sabha*s (meeting of all villagers) also have been initiated to discuss Gyandoot and its services. Incentives in the form of cash awards (Rs 2,000 to 5,000) are being offered twice a year to the three best performing kiosks, with a certificate of appreciation given to the head of the village committee.

Benefits and Costs

The entire expenditure for the Gyandoot network has been borne by panchayats and the community with no expenditure burden for the state or national government. The network has been set up at a total cost of Rs 2.5 million (Rs 50 = US$ 1 approx.). The average cost incurred by the village committee and the community in establishing a single kiosk was Rs 75,000.

The funds for the Gyandoot network have come from existing untied funds available to the village committee, private investment, annual State Finance Commission share of revenues and National Social Aid Programme allotment available to the district council. The district-level coordination committee of bankers has approved a loan scheme for setting up kiosks under the central government's self-employment scheme. Three loans have already been sanctioned.

Each kiosk has a computer, modem, printer, UPS (4-hour rating), furniture and stationery. The first twenty kiosks established by the village panchayat have been turned over to a manager/owner after executing an initial agreement for one year. The village panchayat maintains the building and the fixtures, while the manager is responsible for all the operational expenses and revenue collection. The manager does not receive any salary. He pays 10 per cent of the income from the kiosk as commission to the district council for maintaining the intranet. For the eleven centres started as private enterprise, the owner pays Rs 50,000 as licence fee for one year to the district council.

Each kiosk was expected to earn a gross income of Rs 4,000 per month (50 per cent from Gyandoot services, 25 per cent from training and the remainder from job work like typing). The operational costs are Rs 1,000 per month. The net income of Rs 3,000 must cover investments and provide a profit to the entrepreneur. In practice, the gross income has ranged between Rs 1,000 and 5,000 per month, depending upon the skill and zeal of the manager.

Agricultural produce rates, land records and grievance services are the most popular features of the kiosks, accounting for 95 per cent of the usage. The following examples underscore the benefits of the kiosks to the rural population:

1. A complaint costing Rs 10 brought drinking water to a tribal hamlet of thirty-nine households. The villagers' previous complaint to local authorities had not yielded results for six months. To the surprise of the villagers, their complaint filed through the kiosk brought a handpump mechanic to the hamlet within two days, and he repaired the pump in a matter of hours.

2. Kalsingh, a milk farmer, wanted to sell his cow. He registered with the auction facility of Gyandoot (which enables trading of commodities like milch animals, cultivable land, tractors and agricultural tools). He received four trade enquiries and finally sold his cow to the highest bidder for Rs 3,000.

3. Upon receiving an e-mail from a kiosk that an epidemic had broken out amongst the milch cattle of the village Kot Bhidota, a veterinary rescue team was dispatched the same day. Haemorrhage septicaemia was detected, and the team promptly started curative treatment and vaccinated the rest of the animals against the disease. They also conducted a search in neighbouring villages for signs of the disease and carried out preventive vaccinations. Two hundred and fifty-six milch animals were vaccinated in one day. No deaths were reported.

4. Access to market rates leads to better deals for farmers in Bagadi village. They were quoted a rate of Rs 300 per quintal from local traders for their potato crop. The kiosk was used to get the prevailing market rate in a town 160 km away, which paid Rs 100 more. Consequently, their potato produce was sold in that town. The prices paid to farmers have increased approximately 3 to 5 per cent, keeping about Rs 200 million from the pockets of middlemen and traders.

5. There has been increased awareness about computers and IT in rural areas. New private computer training institutions have opened and enrolment in these institutions has increased by 60 per cent. Around 120 rural youth are receiving training in information kiosks in the remote areas. Gyandoot also has affected political decision making in resource allocation. The local MP has allocated Rs 2.5 million to set up information kiosks in thirty schools to develop a new model of e-education. And after recognising the increased awareness about computers

and IT in the district, the Indira Gandhi National Open University (IGNOU) has opened a study centre for undergraduate and post-graduate courses on computer applications in its distance education programme. The Government of Madhya Pradesh instituted an annual Gyandoot cash award of Rs 200,000 for the project that best takes IT to the state's poor.

Key Lessons

The Gyandoot system helped in filing complaints not just because a communication system was installed, but due to the involvement of the collector (project champion) who closely monitored the manual processes of handling complaints at the back end and made sure that district offices were responsive. The first individual to receive the complaint is a private functionary (kiosk operator) with an incentive to forward it through the system. However, if the kiosk manager were to collect all petitions in a week and travel to the district, could the same responsiveness be achieved? For information about commodity prices would radio, which has the largest reach in rural areas, be an effective alternative means? The question concerns delivery of local content. Regulations have prevented this from happening through the private sector as the government has guarded against losing control over a powerful media. Some fundamental issues need to be resolved before large-scale investments are made to create more kiosks. These relate to the mix of technologies that can be used and the types of services that truly can be enhanced through the Internet.

The awards that the Gyandoot project has received are one sign of its success. But how can the success of such experiments be measured? Will the scheme be viable in the long run? At no stage were all kiosks viable, but within a short period of one year attendance at the kiosks has dwindled sharply to less than one user per kiosk per day, putting a question mark on the viability of the project. Many tele-centres were forced to diversify into unrelated services. District administrators are busy people; the collector chairs sixty to seventy committees. How much energy should be put into technology-based systems? What kind of priority should such projects get in the overall developmental plans of the district? As the district's chief executive officer noted in an e-mail to the author: 'How can one talk about computers when the district is facing severe drought?' There are no simple answers. Perhaps feedback (through focus group discussion with users and non-users by an external agency) from the people themselves is the best way to assign priority to such projects.

Sources

Subhash Bhatnagar and Nitesh Vyas, 'Gyandoot: Community Owned Rural Internet Kiosks', Case Study, World Bank, 2001, http://www.worldbank.org/publicsector/egov/gyandootcs.htm.

Brij Kothari, 'The Moon Has Craters', *Regional Development Dialog*, Vol. 24, No. 2, 2002, pp. 60–64.

World Bank, 'Gyandoot', Povert Net Document Library, 2003, http://poverty.worldbank.org/library/view/14649/.

'Report on Gyandoot Evaluation: Quantifying Costs and Benefits of eGovernment Applications', World Bank, 2002, http://www1.worldbank.org/publicsector/bnpp/Gyandoot.PDF.

Case 7.3: CARD—Computer-aided Registration of Deeds

Land registration offices throughout Andhra Pradesh now operate computerised counters to help citizens complete registration requirements within an hour, instead of several days as earlier. The lack of transparency in property valuation under the old system resulted in a flourishing business of brokers and middlemen, leading to corruption. Antiquated procedures such as manual copying and indexing of documents, and storage in paper forms in ill-maintained back rooms have all been replaced. This case illustrates some of the key implementation issues faced by state and national governments in their efforts to use IT to improve citizen–government interfaces.

Application Context

Registration of document changes in ownership and transactions involving immovable property is governed by the Indian Stamp Act of 1899. Deeds of various kinds are required by law to be written on stamp paper of prescribed value. Certain transactions require a fixed duty. For others the ad valorem method is used, whereby the stamp duty is a percentage of the property value or loan that is the subject of the instrument.

The ad valorem method ensures that inflation will not erode the value of stamp revenues. This method accounts for over 90 per cent of the total revenue from stamp duty.

Registration is carried out at the office of the sub-registrar of assurances. In Andhra Pradesh (AP), there are 387 sub-registrar offices that register approximately 1.2 million documents per year. The work of the sub-registrar is supervised by a hierarchy of district registrars (twenty-eight), deputy inspectors (six) and an inspector general. The traditional eleven-step registration procedure is, presented below complex and time consuming, beyond the comprehension of most citizens:

Step 1   The value of the property is determined.
Step 2   Stamp duty, transfer duty, registration fee and other fees are calculated.
Step 3   Stamp paper must be purchased by citizen.
Step 4   The legal registration document and certificates to be enclosed with the document must be prepared.
Step 5   These documents are presented to the sub-registrar of the jurisdiction.
Step 6   The sub-registrar scrutinises the documents, reviewing the valuation of the property, calculation of stamp duty, transfer duty, registration fees and miscellaneous fees.
Step 7   Payment of deficit stamp duty, if any, is required.
Step 8   Final document is certified by the citizen before the sub-registrar and two witnesses.
Step 9   The document is copied into the register books.
Step 10   Copies are posted to two indexes (by name and property), and accounts and reports.
Step 11   The document is returned to the citizen.

The following actors are involved in the conventional registration process:

1. **Stamp vendors:** Stamps are sold to the public through private stamp vendors (licensed by the Registration and Stamps Department) and at stamp counters located at the offices of the sub-registrars. The private stamp vendors have commonly charged an illegal premium on the face value of the stamps when there is scarcity of stamps of a particular denomination. They have also resorted to the sale of fake stamps and post-dated stamps

for an additional charge. There are about 2,300 licensed stamp vendors and 221 departmental stamp counters in AP.

2. **Document writers:** The document writers have been given official recognition in several states of India through a system of licensing (there are 3,908 licensed writers in AP). In AP, when a document is not written by a licensed document writer an additional fee (approximately Rs 215) is levied at the time of registration. Document writers prepare the maps and location sketches to describe the property, fill in various forms and assist citizens in procuring certificates from various authorities. For their comprehensive services they demand a fee higher than that prescribed by law.

3. **Registration agents:** These are self-employed individuals and firms who, for a lumpsum payment, get a document registered, covering the whole range of services.

This manual registration system had a number of important drawbacks. Most importantly:

1. **Lack of transparency in valuation:** Since the stamp duty is linked to property values, valuation procedures are vital. A system of market value guidelines was introduced in 1975, whereby the rate per unit of rural/urban lands is assessed for all villages/towns and incorporated in a register for public guidance. However, the basic value registers usually are not accessible to the public, and even if they were, it is difficult for a common citizen to read them and calculate the amount of stamp duty, transfer duty, registration fee and miscellaneous fee. All this creates an impression that the valuation of property is 'flexible' and 'negotiable', prompting a host of corrupt practices and a flourishing business of brokers and middlemen who exploit the confusion surrounding the registration process.

2. **Tedious back-office functions:** Conventional manual methods of copying, indexing and retrieving documents are laborious, time consuming, and prone to errors and manipulations. Thus, a premium is often paid for speedy delivery of services.

3. **Difficulties in preserving documents:** The registers occupy a lot of physical space, usually in dusty back rooms. These records also deteriorate with age and repeated handling.

A New Approach

The Computer-aided Administration of Registration of Deeds (CARD) is designed to eliminate the maladies affecting the conventional registration system by introducing electronic delivery of all registration services. CARD was initiated to meet the following key objectives:

- demystify the registration process;
- bring speed, efficiency, consistency and reliability; and
- substantially improve the citizen interface.

These goals were to be achieved by:

- introducing a transparent system of valuation of properties easily accessible to citizens;
- replacing the manual system of copying and filing of documents with a sophisticated document management system using imaging technology; and
- replacing the manual system of indexing, accounting and reporting through the introduction of electronic document writing.

Since 60 per cent of the documents, encumbrance certificates (ECs) and certified copies relate to agricultural properties, the success of the CARD project would greatly benefit the rural farming community. Agriculturists would also benefit from a possible link-up of the CARD network with the rural bank network, which would enhance the efficiencies of the rural credit services by eliminating the need for paper-based procedures.

Implementation Challenges

Implementation of an IT project involving over 200 locations state-wide was a formidable challenge. The project was divided into nine major tasks and sixty-four sub-tasks. Approximately 2,000 hardware items and software packages were procured within a span of about five months through the agency of AP Technology Services. The project had to be implemented rapidly so that the technology (both hardware and software) would not become obsolete prior to the project launch. Implementation required considerable re-engineering.

First, the national Registration Act of 1908 did not envisage the use of computers to handle registration procedures. The Registration Act, therefore, had to be amended, a process that took over a year. The Act, in its application to the state of AP, has been amended to provide for the following:

- Document registration and copying may be completed with the aid of electronic devices like computers, scanners and CDs; and copies may be preserved and retrieved with the same tools.
- Copies of documents registered and stored electronically, retrieved, printed and certified by the sub-registrar shall be received as legal documents.
- The registration software shall be prescribed by the inspector general.

Second, to use these new technologies effectively, a large and well-designed training programme was carried out by a private sector company at a cost of Rs 13 million (9 per cent of the project cost). A training programme of one to three weeks was organised for different categories of officers. Seventy-five data processing officers (DPOs) were trained for six months and 1,200 data entry operators were provided two weeks of training. Extensive system reforms cannot be brought about without adequate motivation within the organisation. The following decisions were taken to motivate employees:

- A cross-section of field personnel was closely associated with the design and development of the software, and especially in the task of business process re-engineering.
- No external technical personnel were recruited.
- The head of department undertook extensive tours throughout the state and conducted workshops, presentations and special training camps involving all departmental employees. The officials who managed the two pilot sites were closely associated with this effort.
- Senior functionaries of the government such as the principal secretary and Minister of the revenue department were closely associated with, and supportive of, the project.

A third implementation challenge was the tremendous data backlog. The CARD masters (state level) could be built without much difficulty, as the data is both limited and readily available. However, the project encountered major challenges in building up basic value data and EC data for the last fifteen years. The basic value data consisted of about 50,000 records at each sub-registrar office (SRO). These data were entered in the systems by the trained staff in six to eight weeks. The task of entering EC data, which has a more complex size and structure—about 1.2 million records of 2 KB size each—was outsourced to five agencies in March 1998.

Fourth, installation of the CARD application software in 212 locations was considered a major challenge. Seven versions of the software had to be developed, tested and deployed in a period of four months to achieve the desired functionality across the counter. This task was made possible by the relentless efforts of the DPOs who were groomed in preparation for this. One significant strategy adopted to 'de-bottleneck' this process was to enable the DPOs to contact the head of the department and a core of technical personnel at the headquarters at any time to solve problems encountered in installation. The CARD project was launched on 4 November 1998. Political figures from each region inaugurated the new centres on the same day, thus helping to solidify political support for the project. An appropriate media campaign was also undertaken to educate the public and thereby bring about the elimination of middlemen and brokers in the registration process.

Benefits and Costs

Within six months of the launch of the CARD project, about 80 per cent of all land registration transactions in AP were carried out electronically. By 2002 all the 387 offices had been computerised and nearly 3.4 million deeds had been registered. In addition, 1.8 million ECs had been issued.

The time required for services such as valuation of property, sale of stamp paper and provision of certified copies of registered documents now takes 10 minutes instead of a few days as under the earlier system. ECs are now issued to citizens in a span of 5 minutes, using a system that searches through more than fifteen years of records from over fifty offices. Land registration can be completed in a few hours, whereas earlier it took up to a fortnight.

Table 7.2 indicates the yearly revenue collection for five years. After factoring out the natural upward trend in nominal revenues, the CARD system has generated a modest increase in revenue.

Table 7.2
Andhra Pradesh Land Registration Revenue, 1995–2000 (in Rs million)

Year	Target	Gross revenue	Net revenue	Growth % (in net revenue)
1995–96	5,700.00	4,602.70	3,256.20	38.30
1996–97	5,700.00	6,058.70	4,351.60	336.40
1997–98	6,390.00	6,359.10	4,496.10	33.20
1998–99	6,750.00	7,100.30	4,935.10	97.60
1999–2000	778.00	786.00	591.00	19.75

Still another benefit of the CARD programme is that it has prompted the public to pressurise government for similar changes in other areas. Regarding the CARD programme itself, the following improvements are contemplated:

- introduction of a Telugu (local language) version of the software;
- creation of a CARD service centre to provide all registration-related services under one roof (except registration of deeds relating to any property carried out in the twin cities of Hyderabad and Secunderabad);
- networking all the servers/PCs at 214 centres using the AP State-wide Area Network (APSWAN) so that all registration services (except registration of deeds) can be accessed at any of the 214 offices irrespective of the location of the property;
- provision of registration information services on the Internet;
- development of a property title database, which would be the precursor for introducing the Torrens system of registration (whereby registration of a sale deed guarantees title to a property);
- linking the databases of all land-related departments, such as land revenue, municipal administration and irrigation; and
- linking the EC database with the banking network to facilitate speedier processing of applications for rural credit.

The cost of the CARD project was funded entirely by the AP government. The 1996 pilot project to computerise two SROs cost about Rs 2.37 million ($55,000). The original outlay for the full CARD project was about Rs 150 million (US$3 million), and this figure finally grew to Rs 300 million ($6.0 million). (This cost includes hardware, software, training, site preparation, data entry, air-conditioners, furniture, stationery and storage media, and other miscellaneous expenses.

Although no one was fired, the new system of post-spot inspections reveal that the new system has not found favour with employees due to a loss in enforcement power. If an undervaluation is discovered, a separate notice must be issued to collect it, and this collection may go into litigation. There is also a need to encourage payment by cheque or electronic means instead of the current practice of accepting cash.

Key Lessons

<u>Clear-cut Plan</u> The government should have a clear, coherent and rationale plan for choosing a particular e-government application. The AP government prioritised and selected for attention a service that generates high tax revenues, has a large citizen interface and some prior involvement with IT. The land deeds registration service is one such area.

<u>Understanding Benefits</u> The question must be asked if there is a clear motive and understanding of the benefits emerging from using IT. Often the value added of technological re-engineering of services is not clearly understood or targeted at the outset, and the outcomes are, therefore, disappointing. In this application, IT solutions were used for the specific goal of reducing the time it took for citizens to register their deeds. Reducing corruption was never the stated goal of the CARD project, nor has it been eliminated to a significant degree. Any government that sets out to eliminate corruption as an explicit objective is likely to encounter greater resistance from employees who stand to lose. Fighting corruption is a fringe benefit of the reform, achieved here mainly through the elimination of intermediaries.

<u>Effective Change Management</u> Of all the factors that contributed to the success of CARD, this clearly emerges as the most important. In fact, when asked about the manner in which he had to distribute his time and effort, the manager of the CARD project attributed 45 per cent to change management, 35 per cent to the re-engineering of processes, a mere 15 to 20 per cent to software and 5 per cent to other factors. To circumvent predictable and formidable opposition from the intermediaries who stood to lose from these changes, the project did not confront them directly, but chose instead to coexist with the old system, thereby allowing

the market to eliminate gradually the demand for these intermediaries. Care was also taken not to antagonise the lower rungs of bureaucracy. The government announced at the outset that no downsizing would result from the introduction of this technology, and is now trying to transfer excess capacity into previously neglected activities (for example, fieldwork).

The AP government has decided that such projects in the future will be led only by public administrators who have been trained to understand technology rather than by technical specialists trained to manage. In a huge and costly demonstration of commitment to this belief, the government has set aside funds to interview, select and train promising public administrators for future projects. This experience underscores that e-governance projects can perhaps be managed best by public servants.

<u>Infrastructure</u> Appropriate physical telecom infrastructure is absolutely necessary for the application of IT solutions, but is an insufficient condition to achieve successful e-government reforms. The Andhra Pradesh Technology Service, a different kind of 'infrastructural' element, was instrumental in the progress of Andhra's overall IT and e-governance agenda. This government-owned company functions as a kind of in-house consulting group for government projects. It is not bound by the government's pay structure, and is capable of attracting and retaining specialists from the private sector as well.

<u>Choice of Technology</u> The choice of software and technology is often secondary to other factors such as proper change management. Certainly, the choice of software was important. However, the CARD experience suggests that its importance for success was secondary. Wisely, this e-government application was designed to be flexible and scalable to accommodate new services, statutory changes in registration procedure and new computing environments.

Also, making a successful transition from a manual to an electronic process demanded changes to a number of established work procedures. Process re-engineering was needed to realise the promised benefits and deal with the challenges of the new medium. Also related elements, such as legislation, had to be updated.

<u>Why Has Tax Revenue Not Increased More Significantly Since the Implementation of CARD?</u> The department has no way to accurately measure the revenue loss in the existing system. Surrogate

indicators such as the number of court cases protesting valuations can be used to suggest whether valuation is lenient or strict. Changing the basis of valuation from the current reliance on historical records (which reflect depressed prices to evade stamp duty) would increase revenue. However, while using historical prices does not optimise revenue collection, it is considered relatively transparent. A system based on market intelligence could use current prices, but would be considered arbitrary unless very well specified. Such specification would require building a GIS database of all properties and collecting market prices of new buildings, with an explicit depreciation rule. A system of that kind will require a large one-time effort, as well as continuous monitoring. One reason why the implementation of CARD succeeded is because it skirted the contentious issue of pricing.

The Prospects of Charging Citizens for Transformed Services

Every e-government project will require new investments. If manpower cannot be reduced, then operational costs are likely to increase as well. In the long run the CARD application may generate more tax revenues. However, in the short term it has been a net fiscal loss for the government. The government was initially reluctant to charge a transaction fee to offset the costs. But examples elsewhere have shown that even very poor rural citizens are often willing to pay reasonable fees for legitimate and useful improvements in services. CARD also began to charge a user fee from August 2001.

The CARD project was one of the first large e-government projects implemented in India. Subsequent evaluations have confirmed the benefits delivered to citizens in terms of transactional efficiency. However, other expected benefits like the gradual fading of intermediaries has not materialised. Other states like Maharashtra and Karnataka were encouraged to take up computerised registration of property deeds by the success of CARD. Both states made changes in the delivery model, outsourcing day-to-day computer operations to the private sector.

Sources

Subhash Bhatnagar, 'Land/Property Registration in Andhra Pradesh', World Bank, 2000, http://www1.worldbank.org/publicsector/egov/cardcs.htm.

Stamps and Registration Department, Andhra Pradesh, http://www.ap.gov.in/card/.

Case 7.4: FRIENDS—Online Payments to the Government in Kerala

FRIENDS is the acronym for Fast, Reliable, Instant, Efficient, Network for Disbursement of Services. The project, initiated by the Government of Kerala, comprises of computerised centres that enable remittances of electricity, telephone and water bills and examination fees under single window. Previously citizens had to make several personal visits to individual government agencies for such remittances. This involved considerable expenditure of time and effort. Government transactions were cumbersome and non-transparent. Besides, citizens had to often put up with the discourteous behaviour of the government staff.

Started on the principle of 'collect and remit' and 'receive and forward', the project serves as an integrated electronic citizen-government interface that seeks to extend the benefits of full-fledged computerisation of individual departments to the citizens even before the whole back-end computerisation is completed. Besides facilitating remittances under a single roof, a salient feature of the project is technical and behavioural skill upgradation of the staff at the centre.

Application Context

The state of Kerala declared a comprehensive IT policy in 1998 with a specific focus on popularising the use of information technology among the masses. On attempting system studies in government departments, it became clear that for any meaningful IT implementation, substantial administrative reforms would be needed first. For instance, it was found by the Administrative Reforms Committee of the government that a single file needed to be handled by as many as sixty people before a decision was taken. In the above context, it became obvious to the IT department that simple automation of existing processes would not be an effective solution. It was decided to adopt a two-pronged strategy—a long-term IT implementation strategy of implementing administrative reforms and a medium-term strategy involving high-visibility people-oriented projects.

FRIENDS is one such project initiated by the Government of Kerala. Like in other Indian states, Kerala has a number of departments collecting taxes and utility bill payments. Individual citizens are expected to pay the tax or the utility payment at the office of the department or agency concerned. In other words, every citizen had to personally visit, on an average seven offices, and stand in long queues to pay their bills turn. Corruption was rampant and the behaviour of government staff towards the citizens not very cordial. Thus, remittance of bills and taxes was a long-winding and painful affair. Customers invariably spent several days in a month just to make bill payments.

Some efforts had been made earlier to facilitate payments through the banking network. However, given the fact that many banks and government departments were not computerised, this effort only led to delayed collections and reconciliation problems. Moreover, only 2 to 5 per cent of the population used this facility.

FRIENDS was conceived with the following objectives:

1. to induct a philosophy of service delivery in the government;
2. to act as a one-stop centre where a citizen could conveniently pay all government dues; and
3. to treat the citizen as a valuable customer who pays for services.

The idea behind opening the FRIENDS centres was to offer many services to users at one point without the customary long queues.

A New Approach

FRIENDS was launched in the capital city of Kerala, Thiruvananthapuram, in June 2000 by the Kerala State IT Mission, an executive wing of the Department of Information Technology, along with other government departments, namely, the Kerala State Electricity Board, Kerala Water Authority, BSNL, Revenue Department, Civil Supplies Department, Motor Vehicles Department, universities and local bodies of the state. Technical support was provided by the Centre for Development of Imaging Technology (CDIT), Thiruvananthapuram.

By the second quarter of 2001, the project was replicated in the other thirteen district headquarters—Kollam, Pathanamthitta, Alappuzha, Kottayam, Idukki, Ernakulam, Thrissur, Palakkad, Malappuram, Kozhikkod, Wayanad, Kannur and Kasaragod. Each centre has multiple counters equipped with computers, printers and an application software designed to handle 1,000 types of bill (in various combinations) payments originating out of participating government departments. The customer simply makes a visit to the counter, fills out the necessary forms, gets a token, comes back to the centre at a preset time and makes the payment for the total amount of bills. In this way, the computer-controlled queue management system eliminates long lines and extended waiting time. The customer is given a receipt for the amount remitted. As the centres are not networked with the participating departments, the printouts of all payments made are taken and physically handed over to these departments for processing. The money is forwarded to the concerned department through proper government channels. The participating departments have the freedom to maintain payment counters in their office premises as well.

The following services are offered at FRIENDS counters:

- electricity bill payments (low tension and spot billing);
- fee for new ration cards;
- Kerala University Examination fees—352 types;
- general fees for Kerala University—ninety-six types;
- motor vehicle tax—105 types;
- fee for licences from the Motor Vehicles Department—twenty types;
- fees for permits from the Motor Vehicle Department—142 types;
- one-time vehicle tax;
- registration fee for motor vehicles—thirty-seven types;
- fee for trade licence—eleven types;
- building tax (one-time);
- basic land tax;
- revenue recovery;
- property tax;
- professional tax;
- fee for licences issued by the Municipal Corporation, like food licence; and
- water bill payments.

The counters also function as helpdesks providing information on various government schemes and programmes, along with access to various application forms. Each centre works from 9 A.M. to 7 P.M., in two shifts on all days including Sundays.

The personnel required for operating the counters are deployed from the participating departments. All of them are given the common designation of 'Service Officers' irrespective of their position in their parent department. The service officers draw their salaries and other benefits from their parent departments. These officers initially underwent a week-long orientation training, which was given in two phases. In the first phase they were given general training on behavioural aspects, such as personality development and public relations, for better interaction with customers. In the second phase general computer training and package-specific training was provided. Apart from the officers, the staff consists of a self-help group of women from the Kudumbasree project of the Government of Kerala. The women provide the necessary auxiliary help for the centres.

The FRIENDS software is developed with a robust back end and a user-friendly front end. The application is specifically programmed to accept payments due to different agencies by incorporating the specific rules and regulations regarding remittances pertaining to each agency. The software can track transactions of remittances, counterbalance, users, reports, bank transactions and also manage transactions of different shifts. Reports can be generated in any form, which is statutory with the various requirements of the MIS divisions of the participating departments. The application is also capable of checking redundancies and avoiding the duplication of records. There are provisions for adding more modules and for rolling back incorrect entries without affecting the database even at the user level.

Evaluation of FRIENDS

The FRIENDS project was evaluated in 2002 to:

- assess the profile and level of satisfaction of the citizens availing the services from FRIENDS centres; and
- identify the profile of non-users and the reasons for not availing the services of FRIENDS.

The research methodology adopted for the study was a mix of quantitative and qualitative methods. Personal interview and group discussions were techniques used for primary data collection. Total sample size chosen was 1,537. For the survey among targeted customers, two wards from the target area of each centre were selected, one in which a FRIENDS centre is located and the other one which is away from a FRIENDS centre by at least 3 km. Five per cent or 125 customers, whichever was higher, were chosen as samples by strict random sampling process from each ward. Data was fed into the computers using the software application Microsoft Access. Sophisticated statistical tools and statistical packages were used to analyse this data.

Target customers were questioned on the following:

1. awareness about FRIENDS;
2. details of visits to FRIENDS;
3. details of payments of bills;
4. cost and time in making payments;
5. location and accessibility of FRIENDS;
6. interaction with officials;
7. overall rating of FRIENDS; and
8. opinion on using IT for delivering citizen services.

Evaluation Results

Evaluation results of some of the important dimensions mentioned above were as follows:

__Awareness about FRIENDS__ Surprisingly, 42.4 per cent respondents had not heard about FRIENDS. On an aggregate, only 31.1 per cent of the targeted customers had availed the services of the centres. Moreover, 24.9 per cent of the sample had heard about FRIENDS but had not availed its services (Table 7.3).

Table 7.3
Distribution of Targeted Customers on Awareness about FRIENDS

Knows about FRIENDS and is availing services	Has availed services once, then discontinued	Knows FRIENDS but has not availed of services	Has never heard about FRIENDS	Total
477	25	383	652	1,537
(31.1%)	(1.6%)	(24.9%)	(42.4%)	(100%)

<u>Cost and Time in Making Payments</u> The average monthly cost involved in the payment at FRIENDS is much lower as compared to departmental counters. While the total monthly cost is Rs 28.12 (US$ 0.59 approx.) in the department counters, at FRIENDS centres it is Rs 7.34 (US$ 0.015 approx.).

With regard to the time involved, 80.9 per cent of FRIENDS users said that they did not have to wait at all for making payments. The average time spent for waiting at FRIENDS centres was estimated to be 5.16 minutes, while at department counters it was 23.18 minutes. Moreover, on an average, citizens saved about 42 minutes of their time every month (including travelling time and waiting time).

<u>Location and Accessibility of FRIENDS</u> A majority of the customers who knew about FRIENDS were highly satisfied with its current location. In fact, 65.3 per cent were very satisfied, while 15.7 per cent were somewhat satisfied. The centres were rated high in terms of accessibility, with 62 per cent of the total customers aware of FRIENDS finding it easily accessible. Only 3.8 per cent said that the offices were difficult to reach.

<u>Interaction with Officials</u> The quality of interaction with officials was examined for friendly attitude, personal attention, efforts in clearing doubts and issuing of error-free receipts. In all these dimensions, the average score of FRIENDS was much higher in comparison to the department counters. Table 7.4 presents an overview of these figures.

Table 7.4
Ratings of Factors Indicating Quality of Interaction with Officials

Dimension	FRIENDS*	Department counters*
Customer friendliness	4.48	3.16
Personal attention	4.45	2.81
Clearing doubts of customers	4.26	3.19
Issuing of error-free receipts	4.48	4.20

Note: *Scores estimated on an ascending attribute 5-point Likert scale.

<u>Overall Rating of FRIENDS</u> Overall, the project can be rated as 'successful' as citizens reported a high level of satisfaction with on its functioning. Out of 502 customers transacting at FRIENDS, only thirty

customers (6 per cent) reported problems after they had made payments at the centre. All of these problems arose due to the non-accounting of payments done.

The centres were also rated high in terms of acceptability and preference over conventional department centres due to the single-window system, convenient time schedule, operation of the centres on Sundays and absence of delay in transactions. Out of the 502 customers, 489 (97.4 per cent) showed their liking for FRIENDS, while only thirteen preferred the department counters. In order to determine the overall assessment and preference over department counters, customers were questioned over the following parameters: (a) absence of corruption; (b) travel facility to reach the offices; (c) provision of equal opportunity to male and female customers; (d) proper queue system; (e) office environment; (f) friendly attitude in dealings; and (g) overall satisfaction. Table 7.5 gives the mean values of the above parameters of comparison between FRIENDS and department counters.

Table 7.5
Comparison between FRIENDS and Department Counters

Corruption		Travel Facility		Providing equal opportunity to males and females		Queue system		Office environment (waiting facilities)		Friendly Attitude of officials		Overall Satisfaction	
F	DC	F	DC	F	DC	F	DC	F	DC	F	DC	F	DC
4.75	3.20	4.02	3.31	4.45	3.40	4.51	3.23	4.44	2.62	4.30	3.21	4.56	3.28

Note: Rankings given on a 5-point Likert scale. F = FRIENDS; DC = Department counters. Figures indicated are the mean values of selected parameters ranked by users of six centres: Thiruvananthpuram, Kollam, Ernakulam, Palakkad, Kozhikode and Kannur.

Benefits and Costs

The FRIENDS centre in Thiruvananthapuram required about US$ 80,000 worth of capital investment (including software). This was the pilot centre, and has twenty counters. Centres in other locations, which have an average of ten counters, have required an average investment of US$ 48,000.

The salaries for the service officers are provided by the participating government departments. Therefore, the government does not have to incur any additional expenditure. However, the following recurring expenditures are incurred by each centre:

1. annual maintenance charges for hardware equipment; and
2. amount spent on account of rent, electricity, stationery, amount paid to Kudumbasree units and other related material.

An amount of US$ 9,150 is spent as annual maintenance charges for each centre, while US$ 7,447 per centre is spent on the second category noted above. These costs are borne by the department of IT.

FRIENDS centres are also used for making payments to BSNL (a Government of India-owned telecommunications company). BSNL does not provide staff at the centres; instead, it provides a transaction payment of roughly US$ 0.12 per BSNL-related transaction, giving an average monthly income for each centre of US$ 250. This is the only revenue-generating activity of the centres.

FRIENDS is one of the largest citizen interface IT projects in India with around 10 million citizens as beneficiaries. On an average, each centre deals with around 400 citizen transactions per day. The gross collection of all the fourteen centres during 2001–2 exceeded US$ 25.53 million. FRIENDS has provided the citizens with a one-stop shop for payment of government bills and taxes. Instead of running from one agency department to another for bill payments, the customer can now make payments under one window, thereby drastically reducing the time spent.

Citizens now get better services at lower direct and indirect costs. It has been calculated that, with FRIENDS, citizens need to spend an average of only 35 per cent of the cost involved in making separate payments at department counters. By saving on travel costs, costs of using agents and related expenditure, citizens using FRIENDS centres make an average monthly saving of about US$ 1 per citizen.

While on the one hand customer convenience is enhanced, on the other hand, the perceptions of the government have changed due to drastic improvements in service delivery. This is reflected in the customer feedback over the services offered at the centres. A few such perspectives are provided in Box 7.1.

Box 7.1
Anecdotes from Client Feedback

- 'Unlike other government offices, this office certainly differs in quality, where attention of special kind is given to every person irrespective of their social and economical status. The interiors are good. The staff gives us a homely feeling, besides being efficient. I hope it continues this way throughout.' **Farida Kumar**
- '[I am] very happy to feel the difference in the treatment to the customers when compared to the normal ill-treatment being suffered in government departments. I am really pleased to be treated as a guest when I visited this centre for remitting driving licence renewal fees. This arrangement is very good.' **M.V. George**

Key Lessons

FRIENDS offered a different model of service delivery in which payments can be made online, cutting down on payment time. However, the back-end processes continued to be manual, providing no gains in productivity. Back-end computerisation of government departments takes a lot of time due to paucity of funds and bureaucratic delays. By resorting to partial computerisation, the government could advance the launch of online payment services by a few years. At best, this model needs be seen as a temporary solution to buy time till the back-end processes are computerised. In the long run such hybrid processes are likely to result in errors.

Along with technology, the 'human factor' was critical for the success of the project. Service officers were trained with a special emphasis on behavioural aspects, skill upgradation and technology. The ambience created the appropriate motivation for these officers to deliver better services. Thus, information technology in itself should act as a mere enabler of government reforms. The real success of any e-government project to a large extent depends on the human stakeholders of the project.

Sustainability and Future Outlook

The sustainability and growth of the FRIENDS centres would depend on possibilities of self-support through income generation. FRIENDS centres can offer a wider range of services and increase geographical coverage. Revenues could be garnered by levying a reasonable service charge for each transaction. An evaluation study revealed that citizens were prepared to accept a very nominal service fee—a small fraction of the benefit that they claimed to have derived from the system. Revenue could also be collected by offering hoarding and office space to corporates for publicity and advertisements.

The state government plans to web-enable services, although web-enabled payment mechanism may not generate a lot of enthusiasm among the general public due to lack of Internet access, usage and fear of technology. Once the back-end department computerisation is complete and the shared central database is structured with linkages to individual departments, it will be possible to provide a comprehensive range of entitlements such as certificates and land record details.

Source

'Information Technology for Citizen–Government Interface: A Study of FRIENDS Project in Kerala', World Bank, 2002, http://www1.worldbank.org/publicsector/bnpp/egovupdate.htm (Web site of the project: http://www.friendscentre.net/).

Case 7.5: VOICE—Computerised Service Centres for Municipal Services

The Vijaywada Online Information Centre (VOICE) delivers municipal services such as building approvals, and birth and death certificates. It also handles the collection of property, water and sewerage taxes. The VOICE system uses five kiosks located close to the citizens. These are linked to the back-end processes in the municipal offices through a wide area network. The application has reduced corruption, made access to services more convenient and has improved the finances of the municipal government (known as 'municipal corporations' in India).

Application Context

Vijaywada is a city of 1 million people (70 per cent of them literate) spread over 57 sq. km in eastern Andhra Pradesh in India. It is a major agricultural trading centre, serving domestic as well as export markets. The local government had an annual budget of approximately Rs 1.5 billion in 1999, of which 70 per cent came from taxes and the rest through loans and grants. Nearly 50 per cent of the budget was used for capital expenditures.

Citizens faced many difficulties in dealing with the municipal government, including bribery and harassment as well as the need to make frequent trips. Several visits were needed to obtain a building permit or death and birth certificates. The issuance of certificates often was delayed with the intent to extract a bribe. However, complaints could not be filed easily and officers were inaccessible.

In paying taxes/rentals/charges for advertisements in public places, a citizen had to visit the appropriate municipal department to get a demand note and then go to the bank to make the payment. Meanwhile, the municipality lost revenue as a result of collusion between staff and the payee to lower the demand, and due to the inability to send notices to defaulters for follow-up.

A New Approach

With funding from the federal ministry of information technology (48 per cent), the Andhra Pradesh state government (32 per cent) and the municipality (20 per cent), the VOICE project was launched in June 1998 and implementation was completed in December 1999. There are two components of the VOICE system: (a) workstations distributed in key departments where the work of the department has been automated; and (b) interface with citizens.

Citizens can go to any of the five kiosks set up in different parts of the city. Some information can be accessed from an interactive voice response system. Those with an Internet connection also can connect to the web server and retrieve information.

The hardware components include four servers located in the municipal office and eighteen clients distributed amongst various departments networked in a LAN. Each kiosk has two terminals with multilingual software. Application software such as Lotus Notes for grievance workflow and a geographic information system are used actively. CMC Ltd, a public sector software company, developed the entire application as a product, which can be customised for other municipal governments in India.

The departments of town planning, taxation, public health, estate and engineering have been automated. Citizens can see municipal budget allocations online. The status of tax payment, grievance registration and birth/death certificates also is available online. Business people can inquire about their tax status and advertising space available for lease, and citizens can register complaints.

Implementation Challenges

Implementation took place over a course of eighteen months. There was considerable resistance to these changes from revenue-earning departments, which stood to lose the income received from bribes. Preceding implementation of the project, performance review meetings were held to make officers accountable. The departments later saw the new system as a way of coping with the pressure to perform.

Minimising the gap between the requirements of officers and the features that were planned for the system by the developers was a constant challenge. Several meetings had to be organised during the development phase to close this gap. The implementation of the VOICE system was regularly monitored by the commissioner and CMC, the system developer.

Data entry to create the databases was a huge task. Nearly 1.5 million records from various departments had to be entered. It was found that the internal staff was unable to cope with this load. A large part of the work was outsourced, but progress had to be monitored closely.

When the system was implemented, training was provided to 220 staff who would interact with separate modules of the system. Sixty officers were given a basic course by professional IT training institutes. A core team of eight officers was trained in systems administration to manage an internal support desk.

There was, nevertheless, a tendency to bypass the system and do paper work outisde it. The commissioner interacted with departments through the system and did not allow anyone to bypass the system. For example, tender monitoring, issue of work orders and work progress monitoring was done only through the VOICE screens.

Benefits and Costs

The cost of the project paid to the developer was Rs 18.7 million ($0.4 million), of which 48 per cent was spent on hardware and system software, and 52 per cent on application development. This is about 9 per cent of the yearly expenditure on establishment.

The benefits have accrued to the citizens and the municipal government. Corruption has been reduced, services are quicker and the municipality has become more responsive. In the first year the system issued 15,000 birth/death certificates, 2,100 building approvals and 224,000 demand notices for taxes. About 7,700 grievances were registered, of which 97 per cent were resolved. The commissioner can view these statistics by wards and departments, making monitoring more effective. Nearly 700 suggestions have been sent by citizens. According to usage statistics till February 2003, nearly 20,000 trade licences had been issued, collecting a licence fee of Rs 9 million.

All internal processing of applications is now screen based, generating greater efficiency. For example, rent calculation for billboards is automatic and transparent; the system tracks advertising agencies that have not renewed contracts; and outstanding collections are sent timely notices.

Key Lessons

This application is significantly different from other service delivery applications, as one of its goals was to reform the municipal government. Reforms of this kind need a champion within the organisation, and in the case of VOICE, success was largely a result of the involvement of the commissioner. Identification of key staff to form a core team, constant monitoring and marketing of the concept to citizens also contributed to the success of the project.

This application is an example of a partnership between federal and state government agencies, the municipal government and a software development company. Contrary to the pattern in many government departments where new software applications have been custom developed in-house, this product was developed by a private company. The application will be quicker to implement and robust, but is likely to be seen as more expensive than in-house software development (which, while relatively inexpensive, may be of poorer quality and reliability).

VOICE was a localised initiative, not part of a grand design in the state's e-government effort. In fact, VOICE competes with an application, TWIN, developed by the state government to deliver some services in the city of Hyderabad. Perhaps that explains why in the three years that have elapsed since the implementation of VOICE, CMC, the private partner, has not been able to implement the project in any other city.

The utility of VOICE could have been enhanced by offering information and services from other government departments like police, road transport, railways and registration. This would require a high degree of coordination at the state level. In the interim, many local initiatives will undoubtedly sprout, and later a solution to link and integrate these different applications will have to emerge.

Sources

Subhash Bhatnagar and Arvind Kumar, 'VOICE: Online Delivery of Municipal Services in Vijaywada', Case study, World Bank, 2001, http://www1.worldbank.org/publicsector/egov/voice_cs.htm.

Vijaywada Municipal Corporation, http://www.ourvmc.org.

Andhra Pradesh Government, E-Government Project, http://www.ap-it.com/itprojects_mar03.pdf.

Case 7.6: Online Income Tax Administration

The manual system of income tax collection in some countries has a number of deficiencies, like cumbersome procedures, poor intra-agency communication and coordination, inefficient deployment of resources, internal corruption and an endemic scepticism regarding the unfairness of tax collection policies and practices. These deficiencies often result in delayed payment, fraud and evasion. To overcome these deficiencies and to avoid the huge losses faced by the governments, some countries are now deploying online tax payment systems.

Singapore is one of the countries where the transition from manual to electronic processes began in early 1990s. In 1992 the Inland Revenue Authority of Singapore (IRAS) introduced an imaging system to electronically process the paper-based income tax returns filed by the citizens.

Gradually, the interface with the citizen was changed, permitting filing by phone, and later through the Internet. The future goal is to link the information in various government agencies related to earnings, eligible deductions, etc., so that the need for most taxpayers to file any kind of return can be eliminated entirely.

The Mexican federal tax administration (SAT) established an interactive web page in 1998 containing information on country's tax laws and procedures and allowing online filing of obligated taxpayers' annual declarations. Now the web page also allows online tax payments and other tax transactions. Chile, too, has moved from a cumbersome and costly manual system to a new system that allows taxpayers to file tax returns online and receive an assessment in 12 hours instead of several days under the earlier system. The Guatemalan online tax filing and payment system BancaSAT started in 2001 and accounted for 84 per cent tax revenues by the end of 2002. The online system has significantly reduced transaction costs and improved service delivery. The system is considered largely successful and highly regarded by users, in particular because of its simplicity.

Application Context

When Singapore became an independent republic in 1965 its revenue structure and administration were similar to those of other former British colonies. The tax administration was a classically hierarchical bureaucracy, with extensive 'front-end' revision of returns, followed by an extensive series of intermediate steps before the issuance of an assessment, and then a separate payment and enforcement process. In 1992 the IRAS was created for administering income and property taxes, and a value-added tax called the Goods and Services Tax (GST). Over the next eight years a completely new administrative system was introduced in a carefully-phased, step-by-step fashion.

In Chile the Internal Taxation Service (SII) is responsible for collecting individual as well as corporate taxes. Under the manual system, a mountain of paperwork was created, printed and dispatched by post to keep taxpayers and their advisers aware of latest regulations. Individuals had to visit their local tax office to see inspectors. The process culminated in a declaration presented on a piece of paper, which then had to be keyed, calculated, verified and paid.

Mexico's federal tax administration or Servicio de Administración Tributaria (SAT) was described as having 'serious deficiencies'.

Cumbersome procedures and a diminished sense of compliance hazard resulted in the non-registration of an estimated 1.9 million potential taxpayers. As for the 7,557,692 registered taxpayers, poor intra-agency communication and coordination, inefficient deployment of human and information resources, internal corruption and an endemic scepticism regarding the unfairness of Mexican tax collection policies and practices, led to untimely payment, fraud and outright evasion.

In 2001 Guatemala's tax revenues were $2.1 billion, approximately 10 per cent of the country's GDP according to Guatemalan tax agency Superintendencia de Administración Tributaria (SAT) figures, and out of the 130,000 taxpayers, approximately 12,000 paid over $8,000 in taxes. The filing of taxes was done through the traditional paper forms, which along with the payment had to be handed to commercial banks. The information in paper forms was typed into an electronic form by bank employees, then printed and sent to SAT within five days, where the information was again transferred to new forms by SAT staff. Finally, the forms were handed to another department for storage and could be accessed during audits. The enormous amount of paperwork at every stage of the process resulted in numerous typing errors and loss of information. Long lines at the banks and complaints were frequent. The complexity of the forms also contributed to errors in the declarations by taxpayers and made the process tedious and slow. It was apparent that such a cumbersome process could not contribute to increasing the taxpayer base and could not guarantee the quality of information stored by SAT.

A New Approach

Governments around the world have realised the potential role of Internet-based technology in improving the tax collection process and have invested in online tax systems that allow citizens and businesses to connect to the tax agency web site to file and, in a few cases, pay taxes.

The Chilean government and the SII planned to start an online taxation package in 1998 to reduce the cost and increase the accuracy of tax collection; to equip Chile's tax authority with the resources it needed for the foreseeable future; and to offer taxpayers throughout the country a higher standard of service along with swift, easy access to vital tax information. The first phase of the new tax service (http://www.ssi.cl) was simply to place taxpayer information online (including the tax structure, corporate topics, guidelines and procedures) rather than visiting the SII office or phoning for a printed document. In the next phase the web site was made interactive and individuals could check their tax status online, which was followed within a year by electronic tax filing.

In Singapore one of the first changes implemented by the IRAS was to convert from a hard copy filing system to a paperless imaging system, which permitted documents to be retrieved instantly from networked terminals. This improved the efficiency of the administrative process, facilitated 'back-end' auditing, and freed staff time from unproductive paper shuffling. But taxpayers still had to file paper originals. In 1995 electronic filing by telephone was introduced for individuals. Legal changes were needed to accept the computer output from an image system as a valid document. Most taxpayers continued to file paper returns.

In 1998 Singapore introduced direct electronic filing for individual taxpayers with employment income. Filers see the entire tax form (including any corrections made for consistency) before it is submitted. If the taxpayer's employer supplies the IRAS with filing information directly, all the taxpayer needs do is to click the appropriate box to submit the form. The IRAS increasingly obtains data directly from employers in electronic form. In addition, data on dividends paid by Singapore-listed companies is obtained from the Central Depository. Some tax information is also reported electronically from such sources as the Ministry of Defence. Taxpayers can use electronic fund transfers (Giro) to pay their taxes via automatic deductions from their accounts. Adjustments in tax liabilities lead to automatic adjustments in payments. Alternatively, taxpayers can pay a lumpsum using the telephone, Internet banking services or, finally, by debit card at payment kiosks or taxpayer service centres. About 60 per cent of individual taxpayers use one of these systems. The IRAS has introduced 'e-stamping', which makes it possible to pay the stamp duties levied on mortgage and stock transfer documents automatically. The system generates a legally accepted certificate of stamp duty that can be printed.

Under Guatemala's BancaSAT model, taxpayers connect to their own bank's web site where they can click on a link to the BancaSAT system. After registration using a username and password previously provided by the same bank, they select the tax form according to the tax to be filed (income, value-added and so forth) and complete it online. The bank debits the taxpayer's account with the amount due. Minutes later the taxpayer gets the confirmation of the transaction from the bank and seconds later the receipt from SAT. Banks are allowed to keep the payment for five days before transferring it to the Central Bank. Additionally, the system allows accountants to file and pay taxes in the name of their clients as long as they present an authorisation document to the bank.

Also, in 2001 BancaSAT initiated a newsletter (InfoSAT) service managed by a private company at no cost for the agency and the taxpayer. The company finances the newsletter through paid advertisements. This newsletter contains general information in the area of taxation in Guatemala and other countries and also technical advice for professionals in the field. The newsletter is highly regarded by the 17,000 subscribers, of which 90 per cent are taxpayers.

Inspired by the early successes experienced by other Latin nations in using ICT for online taxes, the Mexican federal tax administration (SAT) initiated the e-SAT project and established an interactive web page containing basic information on the country's tax laws and procedures. The web page also allowed online filing of taxpayers' annual declarations. This capability was later supplemented by the introduction of online tax payments followed by the following additional tax transactions in 2000:

1. obtaining a personal form of electronic identification (the CIEC);
2. inscription in the RFC;
3. submission of a *declaración informativa* (statement);
4. the presentation of a *dictamen* (opinion);
5. the presentation of a *declaración estadística* (statistical reports);
6. the modification of taxpayer data (that is, the *declaración de corrección de datos*);
7. an inquiry into the status of a taxpayer account (prior payments, declarations, legal or administrative filings, etc.); and
8. the scheduling of an appointment with a SAT tax counsellor.

Implementation Challenges

One of the biggest challenges for the SII was to create a technological platform that would streamline the tax filing and information process while maintaining absolute reliability. Moving from a traditional mainframe computing model, the SII chose a three-tier Internet architecture capable of handling large numbers of concurrent users (over 500 in any 15-minute period) and huge volumes of data. The architecture allows a radical reduction in processing time, and the information supplied can be quickly retrieved at every level. Security and reliability were major considerations, as was the ability to expand the system painlessly to meet projected growth.

In order to extend the mutual benefits of the online tax processing to more individuals and small businesses in Chile, SII and CTC-Internet (a private firm) collaborated to offer very low-cost Internet access to the people across the country, having little or no experience with the Internet, through a service called Republic 2000.

The Singapore tax administration was reorganised and provided with considerable resources to carry out the major task of computerisation. At peak, for example, 200 people (including consultants) worked full-time on the development and implementation of the computer system to support the new tax administration. Implementation of the new systems was carefully phased and monitored, taking into account client feedback in each stage before proceeding to the next. Both the administrative structure and the related process of organisational control, as well as all internal procedures for processing taxpayer information, were completely re-engineered. Substantial and sustained effort was required to plan all these changes, to train staff, to manage the process of change and to monitor it. The project champion identified two key areas. First, to focus on building a team driven by overall organisational interest and not division interest, which was achieved by restructuring units, as structure shapes incentives. Second, to keep detailed track of schedules, Gantt charts were used in regular meetings.

Considerable efforts have been made to keep the Singapore system secure. For example, a personal identification number (PIN) is mailed to each taxpayer, and only raw data is accepted by the system (thus preventing virus contagion). Within IRAS access to information is on a need-to-know basis and is carefully tracked. This feature also facilitates a detailed evaluation of officials' performance. An improved process of data mining is utilised to identify cases for audit and investigation.

In Guatemala, while most companies have Internet connections, most individuals do not. To address this problem, banks are deploying computers in their branches in order to allow individuals to file taxes online.

Organising a team to carry out the project was a challenge. Finally, a team of five people of national and international staff was formed, which guaranteed an adequate mix of international and national experience and sufficient transfer of knowledge to the SAT staff to avoid sustainability problems.

Overcoming resistance to change from public administration and taxpayers was another challenge. First presentations of the new system to the Ministry of Finance were received with scepticism. Also, taxpayers, although receptive, were uncertain of the project's actual benefit. Many stakeholders perceived the plans for a new Internet tax payment system as a threat. This resistance was overcome by involving all stakeholders in the project. Initial meetings were held at several SAT departmental levels to explain the objectives of the project and the benefits from the Internet system. The new responsibilities that staff would gain as many activities were absorbed or simplified by the system were constantly emphasised. These new responsibilities included, among others, auditing and several activities to enhance customer satisfaction. Commercial banks, accustomed to an Internet environment, showed less resistance.

Launching a new version of the system frequently had also a disadvantage. Users noticed that every six months there was a new BancaSAT icon in the banks' web sites, which could have created confusion. In this respect, two initiatives were taken. First, it was decided that the previous BancaSAT versions should keep running as others were added (therefore, BancaSAT2 did not substitute BancaSAT1). Second, provide the adequate new functionality to the newest version in order to generate more incentives for users.

Another important challenge was obtaining the approval of the new legal framework for electronic filing. This process involved intensive consultations with SAT and Ministry of Finance. In the beginning, electronic filing was seen as non-reliable and non-secure for payment transactions. However, presentations on how these systems work in other countries helped to overcome this resistance. Continuous changes among the SAT personnel made progress of the project more difficult. This was partly overcome by maintaining the same project director throughout.

In 2001, the Guatemalan tax law was modified, allowing taxpayers to file taxes by electronic means. In order to identify taxpayers filing electronically, a security and identification password was given to each of them by the commercial banks in which they filed and paid taxes. In Guatemala commercial banks have, therefore, three roles that are usually carried out by the tax agency in other countries. These banks are authorised to certify taxpayer identity, collect tax forms and collect the payment.

Benefits and Costs

The benefits of deploying the Internet technology have been multiple for the countries. In Chile, the online filing of taxes allowed taxpayers to key in and validate data themselves, thereby reducing queries and input errors. To rectify any potential mistakes, the new system enabled individuals to amend their tax returns online. Online customers find the system easier, faster and more accurate than traditional paper-based services. Whereas processing a tax return had previously taken twenty-five working days (still a healthy performance for a paper-based tax system) the new online package was delivering online assessments in just half a day. The SII saves money on printing, distribution and processing time. Moreover, the SII's national network of offices can be reassigned or streamlined.

In its first year of operation 23,081 personal access codes were requested and after three years of SII's interactive services, over 400,000 taxpayers have checked their assessments online, 183,548 sworn returns and 89,355 income tax returns have been received. The Chilean exchequer has collected $1.943 billion through the electronic system. Managers at SII are now preparing the online system for a potential 1.8 million tax returns per annum, plus 950,000 VAT returns every month. The site has won several awards including the Technology Innovation Award from the Chilean IT Association and a Government Management Innovation Award. Readers of the national newspaper *El Diaro* also awarded the SII first prize for the best public institution web site in the country.

Up to 80 per cent of tax assessments in Singapore are now made automatically for simple cases; and the time needed to issue assessments has fallen from twelve to eighteen months earlier to three to five months now. Although staff size has been constant throughout the period, staff turnover has been reduced, tax arrears have fallen, property valuations have kept current and the audit function strengthened. Moreover, public satisfaction with the tax service has improved markedly. In a recent survey, 95 per cent of individual taxpayers, 83 per cent of corporate taxpayers and 93 per cent of GST taxpayers said they were generally satisfied with IRAS services. The *Economist* quoted an American official as saying, 'Singapore's eCitizen center is the most developed example of integrated service delivery in the world.'[3]

The estimated cost of the BancaSAT project is $220,000, spent mainly on consultants, IT equipment (two servers) and small training modules. There were no lay offs as most people were assigned new responsibilities within the agency. Commercial banks, important partners in BancaSAT,

---

[3] 'Government and the Internet Survey', *Economist*, 24 June 2000.

were responsible for the following at no cost to the agency: front-end design, interconnection with SAT systems, security (firewalls, TOKEN cards, etc.), identification of tax filers, agreement with tax filer to use BancaSAT, advertisement and Internet servers, software and communications. The commission paid to the banks has been maintained, and it is the same for paper and electronic filings. Currently, this amount is 0.085 per cent of tax collected and $0.1 per filing. In December 2002 around 9,000 Guatemalan taxpayers filed taxes through BancaSAT, accounting for 84 per cent of tax revenues. As per the projection, the online tax payment was to account for 95 per cent of Guatemala's total tax revenues by August 2003.

The benefits for the taxpayers have been considerable. Citizens and businesses can now file and pay taxes at any time from anywhere. Transaction costs for both citizens and government have been reduced. Operational costs have also declined as paperwork, typing errors and use of cash is eliminated. Similar cost reductions can be estimated for SAT. Moreover, data errors and citizen complaints to the SAT have been significantly reduced. BancaSAT has notably contributed to a 13 per cent increase in SAT's revenue collection from 2000 to 2001. In past years growth in revenue collection stayed between 9 and 10 per cent. From the beginning the project demonstrated the impact that the new system could have on the agency operations. The new system has streamlined many of the procedures in SAT, and has served as a catalyst for improvements in other areas, such as the new system for auditing taxpayers and important advances to modernise customs. For SAT there has been a dramatic reduction in the time to collect filers' information from banks: from five days to seconds. The system has also helped increase the quality of the data handled. There has also been important savings in infrastructure, paperwork and printing. The system also had an important impact on increasing the efficiency of civil servants. Staff, earlier responsible for paper processing, could be redeployed to conduct work in auditing. The increased effort in auditing has helped improve SAT's ability to detect tax arrears and evasion. The reduction of errors in filings has also helped improve the reliability of information and tax monitoring. A key success of the project was its rapid delivery. The project delivered the first product within six months. Based on this, new versions of the system with new functionality were developed every six months.

In Mexico the SAT received 147,405 electronically filed declarations and over 180 billion pesos worth of online tax payments between August 2001 and July 2002. Corporate taxpayers realised a majority of these transactions. Mexico's August 2002 campaign to expand the use of online declaration filing and payment practices to an expanded range of citizens resulted, moreover, in the electronic presentation of 200,000 declarations and 1.6 million payments (400,000 realised through the portal of a commercial bank, 1.2 million tendered via *tarjeta tributaria*). On the basis of these early results, government officials estimate that at least 80 per cent of all Mexican tax revenue is now collected online.

Introduction of online tax practices is expected to result in a 70 per cent decline in the quantity of paper purchased, used and stored by the SAT. The cost savings are estimated to be of the order of 3.5 million pesos. Another goal was to reduce the total size of the staff by 30 per cent over the next five years. The new system has resulted in significant savings in time of receipt, confirmation and posting of a tax payment. The processes, which previously took up to two weeks to complete, are now done instantaneously for a fraction of the cost. The SAT saved at least 12 million pesos in 2001 due to downsizing.

Key Lessons

E-government applications often require changes in the legal code in order to fully utilise their potential. In Chile the popularity of the SII spurred citizens' demands for a legal change to facilitate the authorisation of online transfer of information between the SII and taxpayers. The government responded by making amendment in Article 30 of the tax code, which authorised the presentation of annual reports and accounts and tax returns by the taxpayers on media other than paper.

Well-designed and implemented e-government applications can be catalysts for change in a number of areas. With the success of SII, the capabilities of the system are also being extended to other service areas, such as Chile's motor vehicle taxation.

For a number of reasons, Singapore is unlike any other developing country. (In fact, Singapore today has a high per capita income level and a technologically sophisticated population and infrastructure.) Still, many aspects of the Singapore experience do not depend on its particular characteristics. Strong support from political leaders, dedicated and skilled managers, the development and implementation of a strategic business plan, the creation of a semi-independent revenue authority, automating and restructuring control systems, strengthening the audit function, and simplifying and reducing paper handling through adroit and appropriate use of IT are all steps that are potentially available to other countries. It is important to remember, however, that Singapore's successes in tax administration were not achieved overnight. The IRAS system took eight years to build, step by step.

Citizens acquiring high value from an e-government initiative at a very early stage, dramatic improvements in agency efficiency and rapid delivery of the project were regarded as crucial success factors of the BancaSAT initiative.

Many e-government projects fail to define a realistic scope. This makes projects take too long, limiting their achievements while going very high on costs. On the contrary, BancaSAT was well defined from the beginning and was kept relatively small. This helped set clear goals that could be achieved in a reasonable timeframe. While defining different stages of project development, the long-term objective was also considered.

In order to keep the cost factor in line with the outcome, a more advanced version of the system was produced every six months and launched to the public instead of waiting for the final system with all the functionality. The first version was delivered within six months of the beginning of the project. This, like the Singapore case, suggests that a step by step approach is much safer in such initiatives.

Establishing adequate legal framework is pivotal. In Guatemala it was designed to help BancaSAT reach a critical mass of users. It was important, however, to find a balanced legal framework that, while obliging some tax filers to go online, did not put excessive burden on those without an adequate capacity to file taxes online. However, the current legal framework is pushing to increase the online taxpayer base. In March 2003 every filing over US$ 8,000 had to be made with BancaSAT. Since April 2003, the threshold was reduced every month until August 2003, when every filing over US$ 1,200 was expected to be made through the system. The impact of this change is not known.

The BancaSAT initiative shows that it is difficult to succeed in an e-government project (and in any other in the area of service delivery) if the quality of the service is not high. In this case, the Internet signified a new medium. To persuade businesses and citizens to switch over to the Internet, incentives had to be offered: among others, reduction in transaction costs and time-frames for tax filing and payment, elimination of waiting lines, and the introduction of value-added services such as a tax newsletter and tutorials for assistance in online tax filing. Also, the simplification of both documents and processes is considered one of the main success factors of the project.

The involvement of the private sector played a key role in the success and sustainability of the BancaSAT initiative. The SAT partnership with commercial banks has had a dramatic impact on the costs of the system for the tax agency. The banks manage almost every element of the infrastructure needed for the systems with little or zero maintenance cost for the SAT and for taxpayers. Banks are paid a commission for every declaration filed. BancaSAT is accessed through the banks' web sites, and this has promoted a healthy competition among banks to attract clients. Quality of service is, therefore, kept at high level, as banks compete in order to retain and add customers.

The Mexican experience, like the others, suggests that long-term planning, political support and legal reforms preceding (or at the latest coinciding with) the implementation of an e-government application are the prerequisites for success.

Sources

R.M., Kossick Jr., 'E-SAT: Mexico's On-line Tax Administration', Unpublished case study commissioned by the World Bank, CIDE, Mexico, 2003.

Roberto Wajsman and Miguel Solana, 'Guatemala's BancaSat E-Tax Services', Case study on Tax Administration, World Bank, 2004, http://www1.worldbank.org/publicsector/egov/guatcase.htm.

'Chilean Tax System Online', Case study on Tax Administration, World Bank, 2001, http://www1.worldbank.org/publicsector/egov/chile_taxcs.htm.

S.C. Bhatnagar, 'Modernising Tax Administration in Singapore', Case Study on Transparency and Anti-corruption, World Bank, December 2000, http://www1.worldbank.org/publicsector/egov/singaporetaxcs.htm.

Case 7.7: E-Procurement—Experiences from the Developing World

An electronic procurement system increases transparency and probity by keeping a traceable electronic record of government transactions online. A comprehensive e-procurement system includes three components: information and registration, e-purchasing and e-tendering. However, e-procurement initiatives across various countries, including Chile, Mexico, the Philippines and Korea, suggest that in practice the extent of computerisation of processes can vary depending upon the requirement of different governments. The Chilean and Philippine e-procurement systems focus on the first component of adequate public notification and oversight, and provide complete information on procurement operations. The Mexican online procurement system (Compranet) goes one step ahead and allows electronic bid submission by vendors and reverse auctions. The Korean government has incorporated a comprehensive e-procurement system as one of the main pillars of e-government in the country, unlike most countries where e-procurement has not been a part of a bigger agenda.

Application Context

In various countries the manual system of government procurement often faces problems like corruption, inefficiency, lack of transparency, delay in procedures, lack of information for private companies interested in business with public agencies and so on. In Chile, the Direccion de Aprovisionanmiento del Estado (DAE), the main purchaser for the public sector, possessed weak control mechanisms, lacked a uniform legal framework and was burdened by various regulations of different government agencies. The agencies started developing their own procurement systems and procedures, but it was difficult for an interested private company to know and fulfil the agencies' requirements.

In 1994, Korea joined the World Trade Organisation's (WTO) Government Procurement Agreement and there was a need to overcome the inefficiency caused by redundant manual processing methods. Government procurement processes were time consuming and painstaking, as they required a lot of paperwork and involved multiple agencies. For instance, the number of paper documents processed reached 4 million in 1997. It took an average of three to four working days to process each document, contributing to the inefficiency of the system. The Philippines system also suffered from inefficiency caused by manual and paper-driven procurement processes, which resulted in poor service and low sales volume.

In the Philippines government procurement system the lack of transparency had been a major issue. This was an issue in Mexico as well, where the federal government had little or no information about government procurement. In the midst of the 1995 currency crisis, procurement processes became costly, corruption increased, acquisitions were overpriced and suppliers were getting concentrated in the Mexico City area.

A New Approach

Recognising the potential benefits of information technology and the Internet, governments in the above-mentioned countries implemented a system of e-procurement to address the problems faced in the manual system. A comprehensive e-procurement system includes information and registration, e-purchasing and e-tendering. The Chilean e-procurement system, being operated by a private company, focuses on the first component of adequate public notification and oversight, and provides complete information on procurement operations. The interested companies can register themselves online and the public agencies can notify them about contracts or requirements via e-mail. The bidding results are also available online. In the Philippines, the online Electronic Procurement System (EPS) provides comprehensive online information on procurement and bid opportunities. The EPS is patterned after the MERX Service (the Canadian government's procurement site) and is planned to be extended to support other aspects of the procurement process including direct purchases, bid submissions, central accreditation and payments. The Mexican online procurement system (Compranet) goes one step ahead and allows electronic bid submission by the vendors and reverse auctions, besides providing other information such as registration of vendors, bidding notices by public agencies and publication of bidding results. Online transaction of procurement is restricted, but growing.

Unlike the above instances, where the e-procurement system has not been a part of a bigger agenda, the Korean government selected the e-procurement system as one of the main pillars of e-government. The e-procurement system was implemented in three phases from 1997 to 2001. In 1997, exchange and authentication systems were implemented for the introduction of the new system. By 1999 the introduction of domestic procurement and accounting systems were completed. The strategies for government procurement, business process re-engineering (BPR) and information strategy planning (ISP) for government to businesses transaction (G2B) were formulated simultaneously in 2001. The Korean e-procurement portal is aimed at serving as a single window that provides bidding information in the public sector and processes various operations from purchase requests to payments. The G2B project to support e-procurement was completed in August 2002.

Implementation Challenges in the Three Countries

In Chile, a strong political support besides resources to develop the system was needed. The implementation committee prepared a study that showed the efficiency gains of the new system would reach (at a minimum) $200 million per year, which was sufficient to gain the support of the Budget Office. The committee also sought political and public support through the media outlining the benefits of the initiative in terms of transparency, efficiency and development of the country's e-commerce capacity. Citizens were told that information about procurement operations would be available online for everyone, at any time, from anywhere and without censorship. Transactions could also be traced to the political officials responsible for them. To maintain political momentum and avoid political and bureaucratic resistance to the initiative, the committee created a board, including the director of the DAE and representatives from each ministry and government agency involved in the reform programme.

Developing the Chilean e-procurement system in the context of the functioning of diverse public agencies was not easy. The bid for the design of the e-system was granted to a consortium made up of the largest Chilean telecommunications company, a well-known consulting group and the leading Chilean company in Internet-based applications. Although the e-system's development was relatively straightforward, there were some problems with the consortium in charge of its design. These problems mostly were related to issues of how to reconcile the opportunities and possibilities of the Internet and related new technologies with the cultural and administrative realities of different public organisations and the Chilean government as a whole. Finally, in August 1999, an entirely Internet-based e-system (accessible at http://www.compraschile.cl) was launched as a pilot programme.

After the launch of the Chilean e-procurement system, the role and functions of the DAE had to be redefined. In October 1999, the Government Procurement Act was signed by the president, which strengthened the new system by allowing e-commerce transactions, creating a new and common legislative framework and replacing the DAE with a smaller agency. This new agency is no longer in charge of purchasing goods and services, but supervises the system, provides technical assistance and, for some commodities, negotiates aggregated contracts.

Even with high-level political support, the adoption of EPS in the Philippines has been relatively slow and inconsistent since it was initiated in December 2000. Agencies lack adequate resources to support the introduction of electronic services, as only around 25 per cent of the agencies trained on the EPS were ready for Internet services. In addition, a study by A.C. Nielsen in 1999 revealed that only 8 per cent of Filipinos were using the Internet (although it is not clear what percentage of businesses are online). This was due to the relatively prohibitive cost and undeveloped information technology infrastructure in the Philippines. The Procurement Service Department of Budget and Management (PSDBM) has set up a Customer Service Area and created an EPS Division to assist and answer queries from government agencies and suppliers. Some public terminals were set up to provide access to EPS for those without computers or Internet connections. Still, the issue of accessibility continues to be a challenge in broadening the base for EPS.

Resistance to change by PSDBM employees and government agencies has also been an obstacle. The employees feared that computerisation would result in job losses, whereas the agencies were concerned that they would lose control of their procurement authority and that major changes would be made to their procurement process. Internal and external marketing was conducted before and after the launch of the EPS. Employees were informed that an efficient system would result in more transactions and they would be trained to use the EPS. Government agencies, on the other hand, were told that the EPS is primarily for information dissemination and they would continue to handle their own bid evaluation activities. Support was solicited from the executive and legislative branches of the government, donor agencies and the private sector to encourage the use of the EPS service.

It is important for the Philippines government to understand that EPS is a business solution and not simply a technology solution. Increased efficiency and business transactions will not materialise with the establishment of the EPS if the PSDBM does not improve its overall operations—including delivery time, quality of products and accounting procedures. Initial steps were taken to address these issues. However, considerable resources and efforts are still needed to move the system forward.

In Mexico the implementation of the new system was delayed as legislation and rules to allow new forms of procurement were not in place. The use of ICTs and the Internet on a wide scale also faced cultural barriers. The resources, especially in terms of motivated and trained personnel, were scarce.

From the Korean experience it is apparent that a business culture that preferred personal contacts to electronic interaction has been a major cause of corruption and has impeded active use of procurement information systems.

Benefits and Costs

The Chilean e-procurement system has resulted in substantial savings, creation of a better information market, and increased transparency and accountability in a relatively short period after its establishment. The growing number of requests posted for bidding in the first five months demonstrated confidence in the new system, and in January 2000 the project committee called for further development of the e-systems administration and development to expand its electronic commerce capacities. By June 2001 nearly 4,000 firms in seventy-five different business areas were registered with the site. Although participation in the e-system was expected to be mandatory for all public organisations, after two years of operation, less than 18 per cent of public procurement is notified on the web site. This was attributed to weakening of political support and resistance from labour in the DAE. While the impact of the new system on corruption has not been evaluated, the savings in costs range from 7 to 20 per cent.

The total cost to develop and test the Philippines pilot EPS was US$ 400,000, shared by DBM and a Canadian agency. Five months after the launch of EPS, there were seventy-one bid notices posted on the EPS, and eighty-six agencies and sixty-two suppliers were registered. The EPS provides agencies access to another advertising channel—in addition to the newspaper and bulletin boards—at essentially no cost.

The savings from reducing bid notice advertising in newspapers will be substantial over time as more and more notices are published on the EPS.

The EPS provides comprehensive and timely information online to all suppliers from the day it is published until the bid closes. Suppliers do not have to visit government agencies to monitor bid notices and with the bid matching feature of the system, suppliers can download the bid documents immediately. Furthermore, they will know the potential competitive bidders for a particular product or service. The new system has generated lower costs for the government and increased transparency. The encouraging result of the pilot prompted the government to continue running the EPS for another year from 1 May 2001 to 30 April 2002. In future, the EPS system is planned to be institutionalised as the core information centre and will be extended to support all other aspects of the procurement process, such as direct purchases, bid submissions, central accreditation and payments.

By April 2002 Compranet was responsible for 80 per cent information and communication regarding all federal government acquisitions in Mexico. Online transactions were around 2 per cent of total procurement, and expected to rise. The system has resulted in faster and more transparent procurement and savings of around 20 per cent. Around 25,000 suppliers use the system, and many state and municipality governments have joined it. Participation costs for business appear to have fallen, and small/medium enterprises from outside the capital region could participate in the procurement process.

The Mexican system is considered largely successful, although evidence in the public domain on costs and on key objectives such as corruption or incorporation of new suppliers remains non-existent or weak. The system is likely to have cut prices and costs for government, and has increased transparency. In one instance during 2001, some journalists surfing the site found the president had ordered towels for his presidential palace costing US$ 500 each (around half the average yearly per capita income in Mexico). While not good for the ruling party's credibility, this was a visible demonstration of the increasing transparency delivered by Compranet. The system has also formed the basis for adoption in a number of other Central and South American nations.

In Korea, the public procurement service is fully equipped to carry out electronic procurement services. Online transaction accounts for 87 per cent of all trading activities. Public announcements to invite potential suppliers to biddings, selection of successful bidders and electronic contract closures are handled real-time by the electronic bidding system. The e-procurement system is the first online bidding system in Korea, and is being used by 770 institutions and agencies. By the end of February 2002, 2.92 million suppliers had participated in 20,400 cases of electronic bidding.

The system ensures fair and transparent procurement processes and provides services that are open to all. Procurement processes that used to rely on mail registration and personal visits were computerised. This created a paperless government procurement system as convenient as the e-marketplaces in the private sector. Procurement information including receipt of purchase requests, public announcement of biddings, award of contracts and contract status is provided real-time on the Internet. This ensures fair and transparent procurement processes, and provides services that are open to all. The G2B system is expected to play a key role not only in the public sector, but also in the private sector by stimulating online trading markets.

Key Lessons from the Three Implementations

The impact of IT not only affects the public's expectations and satisfaction levels with the way the public sector accomplishes its tasks, but also provides an avenue through which the public sector can become more service oriented and improve its ability to meet these heightened expectations.

By conducting public transactions electronically through portals, it is possible to eliminate the physical presence (waiting in line, going to multiple offices) that is often required when conducting business with the government. Online transactions reduce the amount of time needed to complete these transactions and the expenses incurred. These savings allow the government to get better value for its money.

Transparency and probity are increased by publishing government transactions online, thereby providing access to anyone, anywhere, at any time. This reduces opportunities for discretionary use of public funds, increasing the impartiality and integrity of such operations. Additionally, having a traceable electronic record of transactions reduces the opportunities for corrupt practices and increases the accountability of public officials. The examples signify that the e-procurement system has in fact helped improve the efficiency and transparency of the process as well as cost-reduction, irrespective of the varying extent of use in various cases.

A comprehensive approach, as taken by the Korean government, which mandates the need to computerise individual processes like procurement, as an integral part of a national e-government initiative, can be a successful strategy.

The case of Philippines shows that in a country with low Internet penetration and undeveloped IT infrastructure, taking small steps with manageable activities within a relatively short time-frame is a safe approach to adopting a new technology. This allows greater flexibility for tailor-fitting the system and formulating a long-term strategy based on the actual experience.

When it comes to choosing a technology or system, there is no need to reinvent the wheel. Customisation of an existing system is often much easier. However, management of the project should be in the hands of the implementing agency so that they will gain ownership of the project and ensure that the local factors are taken into account while framing a strategy. Thus, although the PSDBM based the Philippine e-procurement system on the Canadian model, it considered the local situation and gradually implemented the strategy.

Leadership must come from the highest level of the organisation. The project champion must be able to harness the cooperation and commitment of the different sectors or stakeholders in this kind of project. Leadership by example is also essential. It will be easier for implementing organisations to convince their customers to use the system if they themselves use it.

An organisation must have an intimate knowledge of its target market and know how to segment it. Each segment requires a distinct marketing strategy and also has different service-level expectations. Customers will only use a new system if it adds value to them through the content and quality of the information presented, and if the system and its support services reach or exceed their service level expectations.

Providing constant support and training can be vital in promoting the use of a new system. For instance, the Mexican system included a free national phone assistance service for suppliers and other Compranet users. The Mexican system was introduced in a scaled manner, which, like the Philippines pilot, suggests that an incremental approach builds credibility. It is a better strategy to build incrementally on the basis of what has been achieved in the previous stage, as it allows time and space for amendments to address shortcomings, and for all stakeholders to adjust to the new system.

Political support for the initiative and participation and negotiation among the key stakeholders (within and outside the government) is important for the successful implementation of such an initiative. Political will plays a vital role in the success of such initiatives over a period. The experience of Chile shows that after the initial success, the participation did not grow even after two years of implementation due to weakening of political support. On the other hand, political support in the Philippines is a driving factor in the successful implementation of the e-procurement system despite the dearth of infrastructure and low Internet penetration in the country.

A supportive policy environment also plays a pivotal role in running a project successfully. The EPS in the Philippines is supported by the president's executive orders, which require all bid opportunities, notices and awards be advertised and posted in the EPS, and all suppliers interested to conduct business with national government agencies register through the system. According to an executive order, the bid requirements can now be posted in the EPS and the web site of the concerned agency, besides advertising in two major newspapers. This change has saved advertising costs for governments as the earlier practice involved advertising in three newspapers. The Philippines e-commerce law further supports the EPS as it gives electronic documents the same legal protection as paper-based documents. Furthermore, an Act mandated Internet access in all government offices by June 2002. The Procurement Policy Board is the highest governing body for government procurement. It needs to become more involved with the EPS in setting long-term policy, developing planning strategies and encouraging implementation to ensure the system becomes the central portal for government procurement.

Sources

Estanislao C. Granados and Eulogio Martin Masilungan, 'Philippines Pilot E-Procurement System', Case Study on Efficient Government Purchasing, World Bank, October 2001, http://www1.worldbank.org/publicsector/egov/philippines_eproc.htm.

Claudio Orrego with Carlos Osorio and Rodrigo Mardones, 'Chile's Government Procurement E-System', Case Study on Efficient Government Purchasing, World Bank, December 2000, http://www1.worldbank.org/publicsector/egov/eprocurement_ chile.htm.

Santiago Ibarra Estrada, 'eProcurement by Mexico's Federal Government: Success/ Failure', Case Study No.14, eGovernment for Development, August 2002, http://www. egov4dev.org/mexeproc.htm.

S.C. Bhatnagar, 'Administrative Corruption: How Does E-Government Help?', World Bank, 2003, http://www1.worldbank.org/publicsector/egov/Corruption%20and %20egov't%20TI%20Paper%20Subhash.doc.

'Government Procurement Services (G2B)', E-Government in Korea, 2003, http://www. nca.or.kr/homepage/ehome/ehome.nsf/4f73c10673bbaaa6c9256ce5001fa812/ 4001afb10f2865fdc9256db90002fed3/$FILE/e_government+in+korea.pdf.

Case 7.8: Indian Customs Online

This case describes the computerised system implemented by the Indian Customs in five air cargo units, eight sea ports and three internal container depots. A cargo handling agent can now file an electronic bill of entry from her own premises or from service centres specifically created for this purpose away from the custom's office. The bill of entry is processed online at different workstations. Acknowledgment, queries and status are delivered at the service centre and responses are also input at these centres. The system has led to greater transparency, less corruption and quicker processing of transactions. However, according to a detailed audit report, the project has failed to create an impact on trade facilitation because of poor management and consequent delay in implementation.

Application Context

The Indian Customs Electronic Data Interchange (EDI) System (ICES) was conceived in February 1994 as part of the Customs modernisation programme. The Spery system installed then had outlived its utility and the era of the paper-less office had just started. A system study conducted by the department led to the development of an online assessment and clearance system for import and export cargo. The air cargo unit of Delhi Customs was taken up as a pilot site where the implementation of the import module and later the export module was completed by November 1996.

Figure 7.1 explains the network of institutions and hardware as it works at each location. Different cities are not networked as yet. The National Informatics Centre (NIC), a government agency, developed the software. Their network, called NICNET, has been used for data exchange. At each location fault-tolerant hardware consisting of standby

Figure 7.1
A Schematic View of Customs Online

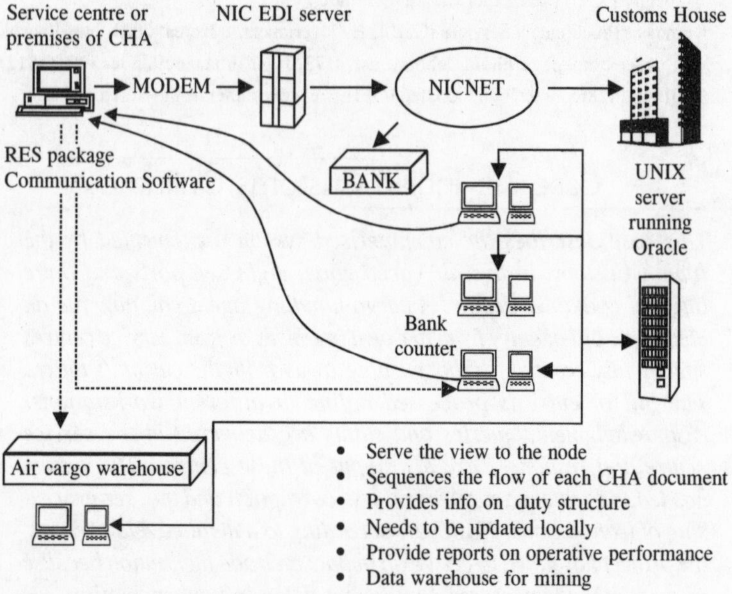

- Serve the view to the node
- Sequences the flow of each CHA document
- Provides info on duty structure
- Needs to be updated locally
- Provide reports on operative performance
- Data warehouse for mining

servers, mirrored disks and dual networks has been provided. The uptime of the systems in five years has been 99 per cent.

A New Approach

An electronic bill of entry can be lodged by Cargo Handling Agents (CHA) from their own premises or a service centre (SC) created for the purpose at a location away from the Customs House. The appraising officer of Customs access the document online and their approval is communicated to the CHA electronically. The system provides for clarification of doubts by exchange of queries and replies between Customs and the CHA.

Acknowledgement, queries and status are delivered at SC and responses of CHA are input at SC. Afterwards approval duty can be paid at designated banks linked with the ICES system on EDI. The only interface between Customs and the CHA is at the time of collection of goods where a concept of 'green channel' has been introduced. The system provides for waiver of physical examination on the basis of the importer's profile stored in the system. In case of export, the duty drawback is credited to the exporters account in a designated bank.

The ICES provides connectivity with other systems such as the Airports Authority of India-operated warehouses, Container Corporation of India, Reserve Bank of India, Port Trust and the Department of Foreign Trade. For a typical import consignment, the CHA has to perform the following tasks:
(The clearing process can start only after the cargo arrival notice containing the Import General Market [IGM] number is received.)

1. Submit Annexure 2 plus a copy of invoice plus a copy of airway bill at the counter and get a job slip containing the job number by paying Rs 50.
2. Wait for one or two hours to collect the checklist placed outside in trays.
3. After verifying and signing the checklist, give it back at the same counter.
4. Find the status of the job periodically at the appropriate counter.
5. Collect three copies of the bill of entry and the copies of TR-6 *challan* and examination order from the printer after the bill of entry is assessed.
6. Fill up the *challan* and submit in the bank branch counter along with the necessary payment.
7. Get back copy of the *challan* duly stamped and signed. At this point, the bill of entry gets detached.
8. Move to the cargo terminal and follow the steps below.
9. Present the delivery order and all the originals of the Customs document in the International Airports Authority of India (IAAI) area to seek information on the location from where the packet(s) has to be obtained for physical check.
10. Get the packet examined by an inspector in the examination area.
11. The inspector, after finishing the examination, feeds the report into a computer. Then the appraiser verifies the report and signs and gives an Out of Charge (OC).
12. Submit paper to the airport authority for calculating the demurrage and handling charges.

13. Pay the *challan* by cash or by debiting from provisional duty account (PD).
14. Submit all documents to get a gate pass. The gate pass is printed in duplicate. One copy goes to the handling agent with loader number.

Implementation Challenges

The implementation of the project has been delayed. Even after nine years only thirty-three of the envisaged seventy-three modules have been developed. Only twenty-three of the twenty-nine ports have been covered. As project leaders and teams have changed, it was discovered that the documentation of procedures and systems was less than adequate.

The department has had to completely rely on the implementing agency for all technical issues. The implementing agency has not turned out to be equal to the task of building a complex system. Security aspects have not been adequately handled, resulting in fraudulent payments in one of the offices.

Even though the top 120 officers of the department have been exposed to economic liberalisation, change management and e-governance in a three-day workshop conducted by the Indian Institute of Management (IIM), Ahmedabad, training efforts at other levels have been inadequate.

The full potential of data analysis for policy formulation has not been made as all the systems are not interconnected and therefore data collation has been a problem. A citizen's charter has yet to be implemented, although tools for measuring and reporting performance exist. The systems run well at some places because the commissioners use the information thrown up by the system for monitoring. At other places such involvement is lacking.

Benefits and Costs

After the pilot the system was implemented in five air cargo units, eight ports and three inland container depots. Currently only 50 per cent of the total revenue is collected through computerised ports. The system was to be extended to twenty-nine locations at a cost of $10 million to cover 95 per cent of air cargo and 65 per cent sea shipments.

A major benefit of the system is that it enables measurement of service levels. It is now possible for supervisors to monitor processing delays.

If an inspector is raising unnecessary queries this becomes evident. The system was supposed to lead to a reduction in processing time. However, actual results have been disappointing. A check at one of the ports found that only 12 per cent of the bills were being cleared in three days, the stipulated time in the citizen's charter.

The system has resulted in increased transparency as all bills are handled on a first-come first-serve basis. Dues can be collected early and payment of duty drawback is directly credited to a bank account. The payment of 'speed money' and collusion between the CHA and inspectors to evade duty has lessened. However, some of the later stages of physical examination still provide an opportunity for interaction between the inspectors and the CHA in a process that is not guided by a computerised rule.

The system can help in policy formulation through flexible analysis of data at the board and central government levels. A tight band of prices for each commodity can be specified by collating the declared value at different ports of entry and exit. Transactions that are out of norm can be investigated. Incidents of dumping can be spotted at an early stage. If tabs are kept on the products that tend to get wrongly classified, a richer documentation can be provided to the CHA on product classification. Exchange of electronic documents with the Reserve Bank of India and other organisations has become feasible. For a while the success of the system in a few locations had become a source of pride for the department.

Key Lessons

Systems that build operational dependence can not be easily rolled back once they are implemented successfully. In the case of the ICES adequate investments were made at one go as funding was not a problem. In other departments a problem of creeping commitment arises as project managers ask for less than what is required, apprehending that the project may be turned down if the entire requirement is disclosed at one go. In spite of this advantage, the time taken to develop and roll out the system was more than expected.

Several success factors identified in other case studies also hold true here. The extent of re-engineering, clarity of benefits and reducing direct contact between customs inspectors and cargo handling agents has contributed to the success. A large effort of education for the CHA had to be mounted. In the new system all information must be fed in correctly the first time. It is time consuming and expensive to make corrections later.

The EDI has not been implemented at all locations, necessitating the constant presence of an agents' representative at the service centre. The web has not been exploited. Detailed guidelines on product codes have to be made available on the web so that items do not get wrongly classified. Independent feedback from the CHA on the performance of the new system has not been obtained and therefore the success can not be fully measured.

The overall complexity of the project seemed to have been underestimated. The department lacked an adequately trained chief information officer who could conceptualise and implement a complex system of this magnitude. The choice of partner can also be questioned. The NIC did not have the experience of implementing a large-scale operational system. The quality of analysis and design were found to be weak. Even though a state agency was used as a partner, the system has turned out to be expensive because of delays in implementation.

For complete success the department will have to see itself as a trade facilitator rather than a mere tax collector. Such a change will be slow to come about even though the top management continuously talks about this new role.

Sources

'Indian Customs Electronic Data Interchange System', Audit Report Number 10, 2002, http://www.nao.gov.uk/intosai/edp/India_Customsaudit.pdf.
'Indian Customs EDI System: An Introduction', http://www.geocities.com/indiancustoms/edi/intro.htm.
Web site of the Indian Customs and Central Excise Department, http://www.icegate.gov.in/icegate.html.

Case 7.9: Computerised Interstate Checkposts in Gujarat

Everyday nearly 25,000 trucks pass through the ten interstate checkposts in Gujarat in India. Many of these trucks are overloaded far beyond the permissible weight. The manual system lacked the capacity to check every truck and often those trucks that were found to be overloaded could avoid penalties by paying bribes. Through the use of computers and other electronic devices at these checkposts, a team of savvy public officials have significantly increased the revenue collected through taxes and fines and made a small dent in corruption. However, the system faltered after the early champions moved to other departments.

Application Context

Gujarat has an extensive road network, carrying a large volume of commercial traffic. Major highway systems link Delhi to Mumbai and provide the principal link to the Kandla seaport on Gujarat's west coast. Gujarat's ten checkposts are positioned at the border with three neighbouring Indian states. Nearly 25,000 transport vehicles enter daily through these checkposts.

Trucking companies want to maximise their earnings from each vehicle. Often this has prompted transporters to load their trucks beyond permissible axle loads, creating a serious safety hazard. The central excise and state sales tax is levied on the basis of a record of the weight/count of manufactured goods that are shipped out from the factory or shipped to a trader. Yet the number of trucks dispatched in a day is the primary basis of this assessment. Thus, by overloading trucks manufacturers have evaded excise duty. (Some estimates are that 80 to 90 per cent of vehicles are overloaded.)

The Gujarat Motor Vehicles Department (GMVD) controls road transport activity in Gujarat. While the broad policies are laid down by India's central government in the Motor Vehicles Act, state governments are empowered to determine the penalties for infractions and procedures for enforcement. Nevertheless, state governments typically have been ineffective at reducing the number of overloaded vehicles. Inspection of 100 per cent of commercial vehicles has been impossible; and checkpost inspectors have been notoriously corrupt. The GMVD department has 137 inspectors, of whom twenty-seven were on suspension (under scrutiny for corrupt practices). It is common knowledge that inspectors' posts at lucrative checkposts can be bought for as much as Rs 10 million.

In Gujarat's traditional checkpost system a suspect vehicle is flagged to a stop and then weighed on a weigh bridge located away from traffic. The legal penalty for overload is Rs 2,000 per ton. However, a fine is often illegally negotiated. Inspectors are also expected to check for the driver's interstate transit permit and that the state's annual road tax has been paid by vehicles registered in Gujarat. Corruption by departmental inspectors at these checkposts has led to harassment of truck drivers and loss of revenue to the state.

The problem of corruption was particularly difficult to attack as the corrupt were backed by politicians. In the absence of any systematic inspection of vehicles, transport companies also adopted various illegal practices. Duplicate copies of a single registration book from the Regional Transport Office (RTO) have been used for many different vehicles with fake licence plates.

A New Approach

When P. Panneervel became commissioner of the Transport Department in 1998, he was determined to introduce greater efficiency and root out corruption. First, he introduced Smart Card driver's licences. His next IT project was to use computers and communication networks to collect fines from overloaded vehicles.

In the computerised process, all the checkposts are monitored at a central location using video cameras. The video camera captures the registration number of all trucks approaching the checkpost. (There are floodlights and traffic lights, which make the checkposts appear like a runway at night.) A software converts the video image of the registration number to a digital form and the details of the truck are accessed from a central database. An electronic weigh bridge captures the weight and the computer issues a demand note for fine automatically. Drivers can use a stored value card for payment.

With each revamped checkpost a ten-lane approach road of 1.3 km has been built to receive vehicles. Each lane has a video camera positioned high on a pole, with a proper protective casing. There is a control room with two servers—the database server that transmits the vehicle data through a 64 kbps leased line, and a video server that captures and relays the video images frame by frame to a central server at the RTO. Power to the system is assured by dedicated lines from the State Electricity Board, backed up by a high-capacity generator and 72-hour back-up UPS.

The video capture and transmit process (known as SIPCA—Satellite Image Processing and Capturing unit) has been supplied by a subsidiary of Phillips. The software for licence tracking and the weigh bridge equip-ment is also by Phillips. The RTO has an IBM server with DB2 Relational Database Management System (RDBMS).

Operators who man the cabins are from the private sector. Although GMVD employees have been trained to operate the new equipment, they are not operating the key nodes at the checkposts.

A database of all the 0.5 million commercial vehicles registered in Gujarat will be created at the head office in RTO premises. A powerful IBM server (AS 400) is installed there with DB2 as the RDBMS.

With the vehicle's registration number, the database can retrieve information on the make of vehicle, whether its national permit exists and is valid, insurance, whether the vehicle tax has been paid and so on.

Once the vehicle arrives at the weigh bridge, the unladen weight, the actual weight, the amount of overload and the fine that must be paid is displayed on an electronic (plasma) board. In this way the process is made wholly transparent to the driver. Drivers hold pre-paid cards (in denominations of Rs 2,000 or Rs 5,000) that are used for paying any penalty. This card costs Rs 50.

Operators also are expected to check headlights, tax payment, etc. Any shortfall is recorded in the computer. Only if corrective measure is taken and recorded in the system will the sensor-controlled barrier allow the truck to proceed.

If the driver cannot pay the penalty, the vehicle must be parked in a designated parking lot. The RTO inspector confiscates the vehicle's registration documents until the payment is made.

Future plans include integrating payment of sales tax on the goods carried by the vehicles.

Implementation Challenges

The new system has had teething problems. The central database is being still built, and it still does not hold the requisite details for many vehicles. Hence, the operator uses his judgement and, depending on the make of the vehicle, selects the permissible weight from a drop-down selection box.

The leased line (64 kbps) connectivity is currently available at only two checkposts (Shamlaji and Bhilad, the two largest). The centralised video monitoring is, therefore, not working properly. In some checkposts inspectors still harass drivers to extort bribes.

The writing and pattern of licence plates is often non-standard and not in compliance with the law. Hence, the licence tracking software has not worked properly (only about thirty-five out of 5,000 numbers were read accurately). Now trucks with non-standard number plates are required to replace them at the checkpost. A vendor is available to make the change for a fee.

Initially the system issued manual receipts with limited information since the automatic receipt generated by the computer, without the signature of an officer, was not legally valid. With the passage of the Central IT Act, the RTO's signature has been digitally incorporated on the receipt.

Data on the number of vehicles crossing the checkpost suggests that some vehicles have begun to divert through longer routes in adjoining states to avoid the penalty. Implementing similar systems in other states could plug the loophole.

Benefits and Costs

Notwithstanding the implementation difficulties with the new system, the inspection of all vehicles has produced a three-fold increase in tax collection over two years. Revenue increased from $12 million to $35 million, paying back the total project cost of $4 million in just six months.

On an average, vehicles are cleared in two minutes instead of 30 in the manual system. Harassment of truckers continues, though, abetted by the problems with the video monitoring system.

Large and medium transport owners are happy with the system because they come to know the exact date and time their drivers passed a checkpost. The pre-paid card means that the driver does not have to carry much money.

However, an independent evaluation of the project conduced after one year of implementation found that the impact on transparency and corruption had been poor. Corruption continues unabated. A bribe of $1 is being charged from every driver and a third of the overloaded trucks are allowed to go without fines. Bribes collected from such trucks average $3, which is only 10 per cent of the fine that should have been collected.

Key Lessons

Although the corruption that has been so common at the checkposts was supported at the level of politicians and senior bureaucrats, Panneervel was able to capitalise on the support of a new chief minister and IT minister who were interested in rooting out corruption and also raising more revenue. He made commitments to increase revenue in selling his proposal.

The promoters of the private sector system employed by the department are known to be closely associated with the transport and IT ministers. In situations such as this, pragmatic bureaucrats have had to operate skilfully to ensure that the procurement of these services is carried out fairly.

To root out corruption, automation has been used to reduce the discretion of manual operators to a minimum. Education of clients (drivers and transporters) about the operation of the new system is a key to stop any harassment. The total revamping of the checkpost area has helped in selling the concept to truckers.

The new system could be used by the sales tax department of the state, which must monitor the movement of goods in the state, as well as trans-shipments. This might require that documents carried by truckers be made computer readable (bar coded). The government is already working on a Smart Card based registration card. However, coordination across departments is difficult, and resisted by the senior bureaucracy.

Judged on the basis of the revenue increase, the application was perceived to be very successful. However, after the transport commissioner who implemented the project was transferred out (in one year), many components of the application have been disabled. The private operators who were manning the kiosks have left as their contract was not renewed because of a dispute on the quotation. A recent evaluation study indicated that revenue collection continues to be at $50 million in spite of the system not working.[4] Failure of the system to curb corruption and sustain itself can be traced to the following factors:

1. The expectation of a short tenure led the transport commissioner (project champion) to force the pace of implementation and complete the whole task in nine months. Even though the equipment to automate the entire process was installed, many software and procedural elements could not be put in place in the short period. For example, the software to extract the registration number from the video image of the plate could not be debugged and fine-tuned. The maintenance contract for the private operator beyond the one-year warranty period was not finalised. A database of trucks was not created because of other components not working properly.

[4] 'Computerized Interstate Check Posts of Gujarat State, India: A Cost Benefit Evaluation Study', World Bank, 2002, See http://www1.worldbank.org/publicsector/bnpp/gujarat.pdf.

2. The corruption at checkposts is not purely administrative and one-sided. There is a clear case of collusion where overloaded trucks like to avoid a fine through payment of bribes. Such a situation requires complete and foolproof automation, where there is no gatekeeping role or manual discretion. Such systems also require a great deal of effort in changing attitudes of affected employees through change management. Intensive physical supervision for the first few years is necessary to institutionalise the change.

3. Finally, computerisation alone was not sufficient to tackle corruption. There was no effort to place this application in a broader context of departmental reform or a drive against corruption within a wider range of departments of the government. The political support that the application enjoyed during the first year of implementation was taken away because of a change in leadership.

In conclusion, the application was focused on the narrow purpose of increasing revenue. It did not build benefits for a variety of stakeholders, such as truck drivers, transportation companies and inspectors. There were many vested interests, which bounced back after the political support was withdrawn.

Sources

P. Panneervel and Subhash Bhatnagar, 'Computerized Interstate Check Post in Gujarat', Case Study, World Bank, 2001, http://www1.worldbank.org/publicsector/egov/gujarat_cp.htm.

Centre for Electronic Governance, 'Computerized Interstate Check Posts of Gujarat State, India: A Cost Benefit Evaluation Study' World Bank, 2002, http://www1.worldbank.org/publicsector/bnpp/gujarat.pdf.

Case 7.10: SmartGov—Andhra Pradesh Sachivalaya E-Application

The Government of Andhra Pradesh (GoAP) has been a leader in deploying e-government applications for delivery of services to its citizens. In pursuit of its commitment to usher in SMART (simple, moral, accountable, responsive and transparent) governance, the

GoAP in partnership with Tata Consultancy Services (with IPR equity ratio of 20:80) developed an innovative and futuristic product called the Secretariat Knowledge Information Management System. Rechristened as SmartGov, the application builds an electronic workplace that integrates workflow and knowledge management in a secure and collaborative environment. With the implementation of SmartGov, the state has taken another significant step in administrative reforms, increasing internal efficiency of file handling processes by introducing the concept of a paper-less office.

In the six months since its launch in November 2002, the implementation of SmartGov has moved at a steady pace despite obstacles in terms of user resistance to change. The chief secretary's office, the chief minister's office and twelve departments have begun to use SmartGov. As per the status reported by the application, 64,118 current and 19,952 electronic files were being processed on SmartGov on 8 May 2003. After SmartGov is extended to district-level offices, it will provide a complete e-governance network that will enable seamless information flow across different units of governance. Citizens will then have a transparent and responsive government interface.

The SmartGov application is also being considered for implementation by several other states in India such as Jammu and Kashmir, Gujarat, Kerala, Tamil Nadu, Rajasthan and the Union Territory of Chandigarh.

Application Context

The Andhra Pradesh Secretariat is organised in thirty-three departments that are further divided into wings and sections. A large volume of communications is generated at the Secretariat every day (the average per day is 2,515 pages). Files related to establishment, proposals from sixty-four government departments, citizen requests (such as for construction of bridges or opening of private schools, for aid from the Chief Minister's Relief Fund, etc.) are processed on a regular basis. For example, at one point of time, during a fortnight, the Secretariat was dealing with 21,749 files of public importance, 10,295 files on court cases, 21,111 files on service matters and 29,438 files on others matters such as audit para and request for extra budget allocations. Information flow in the form of physical files from one government officer to another is massive.

Manual processing of files involves several steps and is a long-winding affair. Dozens of officers read through the files and make comments before a decision can be taken. Moreover, the speed of movement depends on the whims and fancies of the individual officers. Citizen requests are serviced at a slow pace, and often citizens practically move with the file and end up paying speed money during the process.

Files are often opened indiscriminately. On an average 15,000 files are opened every fortnight. Information is not shared across departments and some times intra-departmental sharing is also absent. Besides, there is duplication in the opening of files. This results in different decisions for similar issues. Sometimes new files are created for a consideration even when prima facie the requests are not actionable as they may contravene an existing order or policy. For example, transfers are requested during a transfer ban period or financial sanctions are sought when there is a freeze of funds.

The quality of work on a file is dependent on the experience and knowledge of the officer involved. An efficient officer is one who remembers precedents, rules and procedures. Such officers are sought out and usually feel a misplaced sense of power. On the other hand, errors and omissions in decision making have resulted in embarrassment, such as the government losing court cases. Files have been found to languish for as long as two years with an officer.

A New Approach

In January 2001, the GoAP signed a contract with Tata Consultancy Services (TCS) for a landmark assignment for the development of the Secretariat Knowledge and Information Management System (SKIMS). This was later renamed SmartGov.

In the manual system incoming correspondence was entered into a register, then sorted according to dealing assistants and moved physically. Under SmartGov, in case of a hard copy, the document is scanned into the system. The system automatically generates a number for the file and sends this file to the mailbox of the concerned section officer.

The drafting procedure is now completely electronic. The user simply clicks on the note file link on the left navigator of an e-file and enters the notes under the predefined note file headings. By scrolling back and forth, it is easy to see the history of these comments, that is, the date and time of entry of comments along with the commenter's profile.

SmartGov encompasses an automatic system of maintaining checks and balances. For instance, budget data is uploaded at the start of the financial year and is automatically updated when release orders against the budget for each project/proposal are issued. If the balance budget with the finance department is zero, then the system prompts the user and the file cannot be sent to the finance department. Similarly, if the balance available with the department is zero and the department tries to sanction funds, then the user will be prompted and sanction will be stopped. These checks are done at the data entry level itself, so as to avoid the unnecessary circulation of the file to higher levels within the administrative department.

Other prominent changes include:

- automated prioritisation engine for assigning priority based on the importance of the subject and aging of the file;
- automated reminder mechanism;
- automated generation of routine drafts;
- reduction in the number of steps through structured workflows;
- introduction of checklists;
- introduction of the milestone concept for reminding senior officers about important activities; and
- introduction of form-based decision processing for matters that do not have any subjectivity involved.

Implementation Process

A team of thirty core technology specialists from the TCS was trained at the state government's Institute of Public Administration on all Secretariat office procedures, explaining manual and business rules at length. In addition, several brainstorming sessions were held with the IT secretary.

For each department, executive sponsors were identified from amongst senior civil servants to provide strategic direction regarding the requirements for SmartGov. Department champions were identified from amongst middle-level officers. Data processing officers (DPOs) were appointed to provide support during implementation. One DPO was identified for every five sections in each department.

To increase the confidence and comfort level of users and make them feel involved in system design, information was collected from around

2,000 users. Brainstorming sessions were conducted with each user group that dealt with specific applications to give users a feel of what was going to come in electronic form.

Four hundred and eighty-three applications in the category of core, common and department-specific applications were identified.[5] In addition, an application called the Generic File Processing Application was developed, which caters to around 910 subjects. A human factor laboratory was set up to run the initial prototypes of SmartGov through government secretaries and other users to test the usability of the application.

Change management workshops were organised before the implementation of SmartGov. A total of ten programmes with participation from forty middle-level officers (deputy secretary and assistant secretary) were conducted.

In the next phase SmartGov will be extended to ten heads of department, and finally to all districts and *mandals* (an administrative level below a *taluk*). A unified file management system will be introduced. It is anticipated that citizens will then be able to track the progress of their requests through a single file number, and check the status of the file on the Internet. The GoAP also plans to install a kiosk at the Secretariat reception in the near future. Citizen representations will be scanned, an automatic number generated and the files transferred to the concerned department. The status of files could then be monitored at the kiosk.

---

[5] For example, the tasks in the Information Technology and Communication Department were identified as: training, application to define protocol for visiting dignitaries, monitoring of projects, arrangements for promotional visits, empanelment of agencies for IT promotional material, procurement and monitoring of promotional material, procurement of electronic equipment, and register for monitoring the allotment of electronic equipment.

Similarly, in the transport Roads and Buildings department they were: information base on R&B land and buildings, information base on roads and bridges, processing of project proposals, processing of proposals on repairs/maintenance of roads and buildings, processing of proposals seeking exemptions from vehicle tax, performance monitoring of ports, processing of proposals of RTC schemes, information base on seaports and airports, funding status of projects, monitoring of project progress, monitoring of project progress, processing requests for establishment/privatization of airports, information base on RTC routes, processing of proposals on railways, and processing of proposals for reimbursements from RTC.

Implementation Challenges

The TCS team had an aggressive deadline to be met. Addressing the needs of around 2,000 potential users, the team covered 3,500 subjects, and read, recorded and coded 100,000 files of data.

Employees resisted the change due to factors such as perceived loss of power, fear of losing jobs and problems related to insufficient hardware. The lack of usage of SmartGov by some senior officers sent a signal that they were not encouraging the initiative.

There were too many vendors in the fray. While one service provider looked after network maintenance, another handled hardware maintenance. TCS was responsible for software development and implementation. If there were hardware or network problems, TCS was obligated to ensure smooth running of the system. This took away time from TCS' primary responsibility of fine-tuning the software.

As most users are accustomed to reading paper documents, reading documents on screen posed a challenge. Officers did not get a sense of attachment to government orders as they could not physically sign the document. Similarly, some officers were not used to electronically forwarding the files to other sections as their subordinates had been managing the routing in the manual system. Other officers felt that they could sign a physical file within seconds, whereas it took more than a minute with SmartGov. In addition, typing skills—a prerequisite in using SmartGov—were not easily acquired by most of the officers.

Feedback on SmartGov was collected from participants. For certain features conflicting requirements were received from different officers, and therefore changes could not be made on an immediate basis. Due to the large user base, communicating the closure of change requests was a major challenge. However, now the feedback mechanism in SmartGov helps track change requests, thus increasing credibility and respect.

The timing of the training also created some problems. After their return, trainees from earlier batches found that they had to still use the old manual system since SmartGov was to be introduced after the training all employees had been completed. By this time the earlier batches had lost their enthusiasm and a refresher course had to be organised at the workplace itself.

Deployment of hardware, getting the software loaded into the systems and finally getting the employees to operate has been a difficult task for the Department of Information Technology and Communication.

The number of PCs installed were inadequate. In some departments one PC was shared among three people, drastically reducing the efficiency of these officers. As a result, files were scanned, printed and sent physically across departments instead of being electronically transferred.

Certain technical problems continue to persist. For instance, there is a fear that once the system becomes fully operational, the network will become clogged. A clear-cut policy on space management and archive mechanisms like closing and retrieving the files is yet to evolve.

Benefits and Costs

Benefits SmartGov is a simple tool that reduces time and effort. It automates routine matters like workflow and file numbering, and lets employees perform more value-added work. Time wasted in typing and retyping the drafts is avoided. Employees benefit from transparent creation, movement, tracking and closure of files. SmartGov has introduced the GoAP employees to a corporate work culture.

Six months after the launch of SmartGov in November 2002, more than 50,000 current and 17,000 electronic files have been processed in SmartGov. Further, more than 37,000 back files have been digitised and stored. A knowledge bank of more than 20,000 pages of Acts, rules and references has been included.

According to a time and motion study of the manual and computerised processes, in the manual system a file along with draft letter or order takes 22 hours to complete its journey. But using SmartGov the same type of file should take hardly 2 hours 40 minutes to be ready for dispatch.

Costs The total hardware cost of the project borne entirely by the GoAP is Rs 193 million. A three-year contract for maintenance of hardware is expected to cost Rs 15 million. The entire cost of the application software estimated at Rs 45 million has been borne by TCS.

Key Lessons

SmartGov introduced a paper-less file processing system in the state Secretariat to cut down processing times, improve quality of policy decisions and reduce corruption. Discretion to accelerate or stall the movement of files was taken away from lower rungs of civil service. The creation of unnecessary files that increased the processing burden has been lessened. Time for processing files has been reduced. The process of commenting on the files has been formalised. Access to citizens is still to be implemented.

The system is in its early stages of implementation. It is, therefore, difficult to judge its impact on transparency and corruption. Since the new system is currently not in the public domain, most citizens are not even aware of the changes being ushered in. The current effort is to get the Secretariat staff to use the system so that all files are handled electronically. With such usage there is bound to be an impact on petty corruption. Some monitoring will still be needed to identify the remaining pressure points and loopholes so that these may be plugged in subsequent revisions.

Although the change from the manual to the automated SmartGov system was done to make the task of information flow easier, there was initial resistance to change on the part of many employees. They feared loss of jobs or perceived loss of power due to these changes. Most employees found the manual system more flexible and, therefore, resisted the change to a rigid automated system. Employees who showed enthusiasm in using the system were the ones who liked the idea of working with computers. The introduction of any new system within an organisation needs to be preceded with requisite training and orientation programmes. The end user needs to be intimated and prepared for the forthcoming changes in the system to minimise the resistance to change.

In the case of SmartGov, the stakeholders and the potential users were involved in the project right from the start. The vision of the GoAP towards bringing in SMART government was clearly spelt out, and extensive presentations highlighting the old vis-à-vis the new system were made. Attempts were also made to discuss various issues with stakeholders, with specific emphasis on benefits in terms of preservation of files and other documents, and massive savings of paper. A critical success factor for any project is the inclusion of key stakeholders and end users at every stage of the project. Transparency also needs to be maintained with regard to all-important issues of the project.

The implementation of the project can be considered satisfactory. Currently the average number of electronics files being modified online is 320, whereas nearly 600 people log in at peak times. In terms of buy-in from the departments, nearly thirty-three departments are quite enthusiastic, whereas about twenty departments are not but willing to experiment. The remaining twenty departments are not yet on board. Many employees out of 2,000, particularly in the age group of 35 to 40 years, are not interested, but are pushed into it. In a few departments there have been wrong signals emanating from the top. About 30 per cent of the heads of department are enthusiastic and nearly 25 per cent are hostile. Others are lukewarm. At the middle level, amongst the twenty-nine champions that were appointed, only ten have shown real enthusiasm. Amongst the seventy-four data processing officers, only thirty-seven are really available for the tasks and about twenty-five do a good job.

Even though it appears that the implementation of the system is slow, in fact there is progress because the features in the system are being fine-tuned over time. Since such a system is being designed for the first time and the environment of file processing in a Secretariat is quite complex, it was not possible for the designers to anticipate all the requirements of users.

Accelerating Factors That Helped in the Implementation of SmartGov

There is strong political support for the idea of using ICTs in government. The chief minister takes personal interest in ICT projects and is known to be a serious ICT user. He has staked his reputation and in some sense his re-election on the plank of good governance.

The environment encourages competition amongst departments. There are a large number of domestic companies that can build complex systems. SmartGov was seen as a natural progression in a string of reasonably successful e-government projects in the state.

A partnership was built with the largest software company in India that has the capability of designing complex systems. The partnership arrangement provided a good incentive for TCS to not cut corners in development and develop a strong product that could find markets elsewhere. TCS retains the rights to the product with the GoAP as a minor stakeholder.

There was no organised resistance from unions. Surprisingly, the association of officers played a positive role in implementation and has not created any major bottlenecks. One reason was the assurance that no employee would lose his or her job during the process of implementation.

There are well-organised and trained ICT department to conceive and implement a complex system. In addition, a pool of 100 government officers have been trained as chief information officers in an intensive four-month full-time residential training programme conducted by a leading management school.

An elaborate structure was created for providing assistance and recording feedback during the implementation process. There is a help desk, which receives nearly 150 help calls per week. This is in addition to the hand-holding support to be provided by the data processing officers. There is one coordinator for thirty-five sections. There is a suggestion committee to which written feedback and suggestions can be provided by all users. A five-member team consisting of officers drawn from different departments oversees the quality and design improvements. This team is distinct from the internal team of TCS.

Technical implementers were trained extensively in domain knowledge so that they could speak the same language as the users. A sense of urgency in project completion and meeting project deadlines ensured that technology did not become obsolete due to prolonged project schedules.

The involvement of the chief secretary has greatly helped the implementation process. In two reviews by the chief secretary, names of senior officers who were not using the electronic system were identified and discussed. This had a salutary effect on the officers. The entire backlog of files at the desk of these officers was cleared. It was important that top management was involved and intervened actively where necessary.

The current version of SmartGov mimics the old system of file movement and this approach helped to avoid a wholesale rejection from users. Further, the well-structured note file and the checklist has added an element of crispness to the file that earlier included a lot of irrelevant information. The knowledge bank is an added attraction, though users are yet to gain familiarity with referring and comparing documents online.

The dashboard is another value-added feature as it has reduced the time spent on maintaining manual records like personal registers. The quantum of work at the lower levels of the hierarchy is clearly reduced since the approved e-file is ready to be dispatched unlike in manual form wherein the corrections in the draft order/letter had to be typed and retyped.

Resistance to change comes from the fact that initial efforts required for learning and using the system are significant, and the benefits accrue after a person becomes reasonably familiar with the system. In fact, maximum benefits of the application are in peak load times. The system allows officers to put routine in its place so that a perspective is maintained in terms of backlog and prioritisation of work.

Factors that Produced Resistance during Implementation

The locus of ownership is missing. The project should have been owned by the user departments but the application was seen as an ICT department baby. However, the ICT department lacked the authority to drive such a project, which involved seventy other departments. The motivation to cooperate in implementation was governed by how the credit for success will get apportioned. The ICT department was seen to be hogging the credit.

Real commitment to the goals of the project amongst the senior levels of civil servants was weak. This produced an underlying unspoken resistance to goals. Adaptation to technology also created resistance, particularly amongst the older employees. The quantum of change in the way work will be done is high—from paper based to screen based. Typing is a new skill for most employees. Overall, work can be done faster, but some individual components have become more complex and difficult.

There are many benefits to the system, but not many benefits accrue to the lower-level employees. A shared terminal is an additional irritant. Employees have lost power over information, need to adapt to a completely different way of work and can be subject to scrutiny, without any compensating gains. Although extensive training was provided to each employee, the timing was not always right and the bosses were not involved.

Regarding the mechanism of departmental troubleshooters and departmental champions, only 30 to 40 per cent of the identified people were capable of performing these roles effectively.

The greatest challenge for the GoAP is sustainability. The GoAP lacks the network bandwidth for implementation and cannot be sure of the situation five years from now when the application is deployed at many more offices.

Future Issues and Some Ways in Which Resistance Can be Minimised

In order to increase the usage of the SmartGov system, certain mandatory procedures could be introduced. For example, processing of all employee-related issues like sanction of leave, loans and advances, medical reimbursement, etc., may be compulsorily done through SmartGov. Senior officers should refuse to see a physical file except in subjects like vigilance inquiry cases or court cases where for reasons of confidentiality it is still proposed to continue with paper files.

SmartGov operates in a collaborative environment. Inaction from a single point in the workflow can result in a deadlock. Therefore, keeping each individual motivated is key to the overall effectiveness of the system. SmartGov has to be popularised further by developing an informal competition among departments in terms of adapting the system. Awarding prizes and incentives to departments that use the system regularly and effectively could do this. TCS is trying to win over users by making the system greet users on their birthdays. Perhaps intimation about the birthday of an employee could be sent to all other employees in a particular department. This may generate team spirit.

SmartGov would have a better citizen interface if all government orders pertaining to common issues are automatically uplinked to other government portals like AP online. The citizen will then have access to government orders instantaneously, which is one of the key factors of transparency in SMART government.

Some applications in SmartGov can be further simplified to increase its acceptability. For instance, if a current forms a part of an existing file then the section officer has to search for files, attach this current to the relevant file and then send it to the assistant section officer. Many section officer's find this process cumbersome. This process can easily be automated by introducing an additional field for indicating the number of the existing file to which the current should be automatically attached.

A clear fall out of SmartGov is that *attendants and personal assistants/ secretaries* have no role to play in the electronic processing of files. Either their jobs need to be redefined or they have to be redeployed elsewhere.

The following organisational arrangement can strengthen the internal implementation team and facilitate an easy phase-out of the TCS team:

- subject matter experts who can be made responsible for the implementation tasks;
- a technology management group and a data management group for organisational support and knowledge upgradation;
- a system administrator; and

- a full-time qualified DPO in each department who can take over the tasks currently being performed by TCS professionals, such as those involving change of ID or change of subjects when employees are transferred.

A cautious approach is being followed for expansion of the project. Once the implementation of SmartGov reaches all levels at the Secretariat, it will be replicated in other places. It is proposed to expand it to heads of departments, districts and *mandals*. But while doing so, further simplification, standardisation and replication of successes is needed.

The government has not yet appointed a project manager for SmartGov. Even among the DPOs and department champions, only 30 per cent are effective and they only react to a situation. They do not have a regular job chart to check systems on a daily routine. Instead, they wait till a user calls up and then attend to the problem.

The government needs to find real champions in key departments for sending out the message that it is keen on implementing its SMART vision. Identifying these champions is difficult in an environment where everyone feels they are the first among equals.

To tide over some of these problems, a core group was set up in February 2003. This group has to meet every Monday to review the situation. But is it neither meeting as per schedule, nor are its decisions being conveyed to the entire Secretariat.

A new chief secretary took charge on 31 March 2003. The slow adoption of the new system continues to be a concern. The benefits of the system have largely not been realised either by the government or the citizens. It is difficult to predict whether this system will ever get incorporated into the work culture of the secretariat—to an extent that it can be sustained under any leadership.

Source

Subhash Bhatnagar, A. Vijay Lakshmi and R. Padma, 'SmartGov: Andhra Pradesh Sachivalaya E-Application', Case prepared for the E-Government and Civil Service Project, Public Sector Group, PREM Network, World Bank, October 2003.

Case 7.11: OPEN—Seoul's Anti-Corruption Project

The OPEN (Online Procedures Enhancement for Civil Applications) system of Seoul municipality exemplifies the impact of making decision-making processes and actions of individual civil servants transparent. The system publishes a variety of information related to the services, permits and licences issued by the local government. The status of an application can be tracked by the applicant on a web site. Extensive municipal regulations, spurred by the expansion of the municipal bureaucracy, had created new opportunities for corruption. In 1998, the mayor of the city declared an all-out war on corruption through preventive and punitive measures, increased transparency in administration and enhanced public–private partnership. Some other measures introduced prior to computer-isation included simplifying regulations and actively involving citizens in various anti-corruption activities. The system was recognised as a 'Good Practice' at the Ninth International Anti-Corruption Conference in Durban, South Africa, in 1999.

Application Context

Seoul, the capital of the Republic of Korea, has a population of over 10 million. Rapid economic growth has been accompanied by an expansion of the municipal bureaucracy. However, extensive municipal regulations also created new opportunities for corruption. Some bribes were meant to be insurance fees to avoid unfavourable treatment, others were honorariums for preferential treatment, and still others were express fees to facilitate speedy processing.

A New Approach

With the inauguration of Mayor Goh in 1998, Seoul declared an all-out war on corruption. Deregulation has been a core element of the action plan. By May 2000, 392 municipal regulations had been eliminated, 203 were eased and another 3,897 improved.

To minimise the potential for collusion, the long-standing practice of assigning to one individual jurisdiction over permits, approvals or inspections within a particular geographic area was abolished. Officials are now assigned on a daily basis to handle applications submitted from different areas.

For a direct and convenient interface with citizens, the Seoul municipal government created an Internet portal. It was called Online Procedures Enhancement for Civil Applications (OPEN), symbolising that it opens up administrative procedures to the public. The portal explains the various elements of the anti-corruption drive, displays an anti-corruption index and survey results, educates citizens on rules and procedures, and enables a real-time monitoring of the progress of an application for a permit or licence.

A review team comprising of staff experienced in audit and inspection was set up on 1 Februray 1999 to determine which municipal government activities should be made open to the public. The team analysed the entire array of civil permits and approvals by title, processing procedures, corruption-prone factors and types of irregularities. The twenty-six categories of civil applications published on the web are those that most frequently cause irregularities, cause inconvenience to citizens due to the complexity of the processing procedure, and those whose publication is expected to curb requests for concessions.

Information about required paperwork and how applications are processed are provided on the web for each procedure. The system also includes information on the city department in charge, the staff in charge and a telephone number. All application documents provide an e-mail address at the bottom so that people may easily ask questions or make comments directly.

The OPEN system requires that at each review stage, the relevant official input the date and time when each application is processed. Free access to the status of an application makes applicants feel no need to contact officials or to provide a bribe to complete the process.

Return postcards are sent to those who have applied for permits or approvals from the municipal government, ensuring some feedback. The results of these surveys form part of a new 'Anti-Corruption Index' (ACI). Additional channels of direct dialogue have been opened between citizens and the mayor. Examples include hotlines, e-mails and the 'Mayor's Saturday Date with Citizens' programme.

Implementation Challenges

A total of 5,000 employees in 485 city departments dealing with various applications were trained in computer rooms to operate the system, and add and change data. Following training, IDs and passwords were assigned to allow each individual trainee to make entries at his or her department.

From July 2000, more government functions will be made public, including twenty more civil affairs functions in areas such as sanitation, welfare, construction, housing, urban planning and fire-fighting.

Benefits and Costs

In the first thirteen months of the OPEN system, civil applications published by each city department totalled 28,000, and the number of visits to the OPEN site reached 2 million by the end of the year 2000.[6] The general public's interest in the site has been increased to an average of 1,600 visits a day. Results from a survey of 1,245 citizens showed that 84.3 per cent believed that OPEN led to greater transparency. Other surveys conducted by the local chapter of Transparency International in 2000 and 2001 indicated a growing interest, but a marginal decline in user satisfaction over time.[7] There was little change in the perceived benefits of reduced time or easy access. However, the percentage of respondents identifying greater transparency (25.1 per cent in 2000) and prevention of corruption (9.3 per cent in 2000) as benefits did go down over this time period by 3.3 and 1.4 per cent respectively.

A total of eighty-three corrupt practices by civil servants were reported by the investigation organisations in 1998. However, not a single case had been filed since February 2000, after which the full-fledged anti-corruption programmes were implemented. A survey by the audit and inspection division of those seeking services from the city government showed that favourable opinions about the kindness of civil servants increased significantly from 54.8 per cent in December 1998 to 71.2 per cent in June 1999.

Key Lessons

The focus of the anti-corruption programme was not on IT but on simplification of regulations and procedures, re-engineering of work practices,

[6] Hong Bin Kang, 'Cleaning up the City Government of Seoul: A Systemic Approach', Paper Presented at the second annual Conference of the ADB/OECD on Combating Corruption in the Asia Pacific Region, Seoul Office of the Prime Minister, Seoul, 11–13 December 2000, pp. 5–6.

[7] Transparency International Korea, 'Special Report: Survey of Seoul City's OPEN System', newsletter, June 2001, http://ti.or.kr. The percentage of respondents (from a random sample of 1,000) familiar with OPEN grew by 19 percentage points to 74 per cent. Nearly 90 per cent intend to use (up by 20 per cent) OPEN in future, while actual users grew to 16 per cent of respondents (up by 5 percentage points). The proportion of satisfied users declined from 56 to 48 per cent, and the proportion of dissatisfied users grew marginally to 9 per cent.

transparency in procedures and effective communication with citizens. Technology simply has been an enabler, particularly in building a transparent tracking system for permit and licence applications.

Commitment from the top (in this case the mayor) was an important reason for the success of the OPEN initiative, as adequate resources were provided for the IT project and there was significant participation from the line management in carrying out systems analysis.

Sources

Case Study on OPEN, Seoul's Anti-Corruption Project, World Bank, 2000, http://www1. worldbank.org/publicsector/egov/seoulcs.htm.

Web site OPEN, http://english.metro.seoul.kr/government/policies/anti/civilapplications/.

S.C. Bhatnagar, 'Access to Information Report: E-Government', in Robin Hodess, Tania Inowlocki and Toby Wolfe (eds), *Global Corruption Report 2003*. London: Profile Books, 2003, http://www.globalcorruptionreport.org/.

Case 7.12: The Central Vigilance Commission Web Site—A Bold Anti-Corruption Experiment

In an effort to propagate the idea of zero tolerance for corruption, the Central Vigilance Commission (CVC) in India has begun to share with citizens a large amount of information related to corruption. The CVC web site has published the names of officers from the elite administrative and revenue services against whom investigations have been ordered or penalties imposed for corruption. Newsweek *magazine carried an article about this effort, calling it 'e-shame'. The web site helped in bringing the issue of corruption centrestage in the Indian media for a while. Some aspects of the web site attracted disproportionate media attention, diluting the overall impact that the web site could have had.*

Application Context

In the Transparency International rankings for 1999, India was placed seventy-third among the ninety-nine countries rated. Corruption flourishes in India because it is perceived to be a low-risk, high-profit business. In service delivery, there is a lack of transparency in rules and procedures, and significant delays in operations or functioning. The lack of transparency provides an opportunity for public servants to mislead citizens who have to transact business with them, and extract bribes.

Certainly, the size of India's parallel economy (or black market), estimated at 40 per cent of GDP, provides fertile ground for corruption to flourish. Equally important, the corrupt face little deterrence. There are enormous delays in the prosecution of cases in courts. What is worse, the conviction rate is hardly 6 per cent in criminal cases.

There is a perception that corruption begins at the top, but senior bureaucrats are never investigated or punished. The main investigating agency, the Central Bureau of Investigation (CBI), has limited credibility in the eyes of the public.

The Central Vigilance Commission was set up in 1964 as a government agency. Vigilance commissions and institutions called Lok Ayukta have also been set up and in some states. These institutions are generally headed by retired public servants or high court judges. Their effectiveness has been mixed.

A New Approach

In 1998, based on the directive of the Supreme Court, the government converted the CVC into a statutory body through an executive order. (A bill to formalise the statutory existence of the commission was under the consideration of a select committee of the Indian Parliament in 2001.) The newly independent commission has taken several initiatives, particularly in recommending the use of IT by banks and other public institutions to bring in transparency.

One of the initiatives was the creation of a web site, and one of its first actions (January 2000) was to publish the names of senior officers who were charged with violating conduct rules. The CVC web site contains the following sections/features through which the CVC communicates with the public:

1. The commission informs the public about its role, responsibility and strategies to combat corruption. This is an effort to keep the agenda of fighting corruption alive in the public mind.
2. The commissioner communicates directly with the public through messages and speeches to bolster confidence in the institution.

3. There are instructions on how any citizen can lodge a complaint against corruption, without fear of disclosure or reprisal.
4. There is a Central Vigilance Officer's List, where each organisation listed is expected to nominate a senior officer to whom an employee can take a complaint on corruption.
5. There is statistical reporting of the achievements of the commission (annual report).

Details of convictions of public servants by the courts are also presented, along with information on officers from the all-India services against whom an enquiry has been initiated or a penalty imposed. This section also highlights the performance of various departments responsible for conducting investigations.

Although the public at large often knows who is a corrupt public servant, there has been no systematic method by which this information could be brought to the notice of either the CBI or the Income Tax Department. A new feature of the CVC site will now increase the risk element for the corrupt, whose ill-gotten wealth is stashed away in the form of black money, foreign accounts, *benami* bank accounts (wealth hidden under false names), jewellery and other valuables, *benami* (in a false name) property, etc. Members of public can now report against a public servant about possession of black money or assets believed to be disproportionate to his known sources of income. The CVC will scrutinise the information so received, and if the information is considered sufficient for carrying out detailed investigations, the CBI or the income tax authorities will be advised accordingly.

The CVC clearly states that it does not entertain anonymous or pseudonymous complaints. However, the identity of the complainant can be protected if he/she so desires. Section 182 of the Indian Penal Code makes it a criminal offence for a person to report to a public servant any information that he/she knows or believes to be false.

The CBI and the Income Tax Department have schemes under which informants are rewarded for the information they provide. The informants who provide information under CVC notification are also eligible for such rewards.

Implementation Challenges

The display of names of senior officials of the government, including Indian Administrative Service (IAS) and Indian Police Service (IPS) officers, on the CVC web site in January 2000 caused a mild furore in the media. According to the CVC, the publication of these names was intended to meet a long-standing demand of the media for information about senior officials facing corruption charges and inquires. The general perception of the public was that this kind of negative publicity appeared only against mid-level or junior officials. Over 90 per cent of those polled by the *Hindustan Times* welcomed the action. However, some newspapers decried the publication of the list in their editorials. Many citizens would conclude that a person is corrupt if their name appears on the web site. But, in fact, only an inquiry had been ordered, which might ultimately exonerate the person.

One of the IAS associations passed a resolution against the CVC stating that publication of a name on the site could bias the process of departmental inquiry/action. Under the law, no defamation has been caused by publicising the names of the charged officers; yet the general perception seemed to be that the CVC web site exposed a kind of a rogues' gallery.

In response to these criticisms, the CVC argued that all it had done was to extend to the departmental inquiries a practice that is as old as the Indian Penal Code in criminal cases. Under criminal law, when a person is accused he is legally innocent until proven guilty, but the name of the accused enters the public domain.

Benefits and Costs

Some of the officers whose names appeared on the CVC web site occupied sensitive positions in government. It is a common principle in government that if a person is facing a vigilance inquiry, he should not be placed in a sensitive post. However, this practice was not being followed in India. That is one reason why corruption has flourished in the system. The CVC site brought this issue to the fore.

Another positive outcome from the site is that several people whose names appeared complained that they had never even been served with a chargesheet. Lengthy delays in the conduct of a departmental inquiry also help corruption to flourish. Delays provide a cover of respectability for the guilty. Worse perhaps is that if departmental inquires are delayed, an innocent person may become a victim of mindless departmental procedure. His career may be ruined due to delays in getting his name cleared. The CVC now sends a monthly reminder to all departmental authorities so that the disposal of the cases may be expedited. The CVC aims to have all departmental inquires completed within six months.

The question may be raised whether in a country like India, with a low computer density, a web site like the CVC's can be an effective anti-corruption tool. By September 2001, only 150,000 hits had been registered on the site. Fortunately, India has a free and vibrant press. Both the print and electronic media have been able to transmit the content of the CVC web site throughout the country. Thus, the site has had a much bigger impact than what could be expected based on India's computer density alone.

Key Lessons

Although a large volume of information is available on the CVC web site, only certain specifics were picked up by the media. The publication of the names of highly-placed members of government attracted significant media attention. However, when sensitive information is shared, the media must also have the ability to analyse and draw conclusions. The media will need to be educated (and educate themselves) in order to perform such a role effectively.

The CVC experiment may embolden other agencies like public banks to publish the names of wilful defaulters. The governor of the Reserve Bank of India has announced that the Bank would examine this issue. Similarly, there were reports that the Department of Company Affairs was thinking of publishing the names of its defaulters.

Despite the fact that Indian society has become insensitive and cynical about corruption, the web site seemed to cause some stirring of conscience. Officers whose names were published were indeed shamed. In an article, the CVC commissioner noted that some of these officers came and cried before him saying that their children were asking why their names were on the web site. A poll by the *Economic Times*, a leading financial daily in India, reported that 83 per cent of respondents believed that publishing the names of charged officers on the CVC web site will have a deterrent effect on corruption.

Other web sites run by Indian NGOs have begun to focus on corruption. For example, Tehelka.com exposed a major bribery scandal in the defence department by publishing a secretly filmed video clip on its web site. Overall, web publishing has emerged as an interesting new instrument to promote greater transparency and improved governance.

Sources

Subhash Bhatnagar, 'CVC Web Site: A Bold Experiment in Anti-Corruption', Case Study, World Bank, 2001, http://www1.worldbank.org/publicsector/egov/cvc_cs.htm.

Web site of the Central Vigilance Commision, http://www.cvc.nic.in/.

Bibliography

Accenture, 'Governments Closing Gap Between Political Rhetoric and e-Government Reality', 2001, http://www.accenture.com/xd/xd.asp?it=enWeb&xd=industries/government/ gove_study.xml.

Anthony, Elias Tsougranis, 'Measuring Informatization: A Longitudinal Cross-national Exploration', doctoral dissertation, Maxwell School, Syracuse University, New York.

Bellamy, C. and **J.A. Taylor,** *Governing in the Information Age.* Buckingham and Philadelphia, PA: Open University Press, 1998.

Berman, B.J. and **W.J. Tettey,** 'African States, Bureaucratic Culture and Computer Fixes', *Public Administration and Development*, Vol. 21, No. 1, 2001, pp. 1–13.

Bhatia, Bela and **J. Drèze,** 'Campaign in Rural India: Freedom of Information is Key to Anti-Corruption Campaign'. Berlin: Transparency International, 1998, http://www.transparency.org/documents/work-papers/bhatia-dreze.html.

Bhatnagar, S.C., 'E-Government: Transparency and Corruption—Does E-Government Help?', Commonwealth Human Rights Initiative Report for CHOGM, 2003.

———, 'E-Government: Lessons from Implementation in Developing Countries', *Regional Development Dialog*, Vol. 24, Autumn, 2002, pp. 164–73.

———, 'Access to Information Report: E-Government', in Robin Hodess, Tania Inowlocki and Toby Wolfe (eds), *Global Corruption Report*. London: Profile Books, 2003, pp. 24–32.

Boyoung, Im and **Jung Jinwoo,** 'Strengthening Government—Citizen Connections: Using ICTs to Strengthen Government Transparency and Relations with Citizens In Korea', draft prepared for OECD, Korean Ministry of Planning and Budget and Seoul National University, Seoul, 2001.

Byungtae, Kang, 'Anti-Corruption Measures in the Public Procurement Service Sector in Korea', paper presented at the Asia Pacific Forum on Combating Corruption, Seoul, Korea, December 2000.

Cheung, A., 'Efficiency as the Rhetoric? Public-sector Reform in Hong Kong Explained', *International Review of Administrative Sciences*, Vol. 62, No. 1, 1996, pp. 31–47.

Fritz, Machlup, *The Production and Distribution of Knowledge in the United States.* Princeton, NJ: Princeton University Press, 1962.

Gosling, P., *Government in the Digital Age.* London: Bowerdean, 1997.

Government of India, 'Information Technology Action Plan: IT for All Indians by 2008', http://it-taskforce.nic.in.

Government of Malaysia, 'Malaysian Administrative Modernization and Management Planning Unit', E-Government Flagship Application, 2003, http://www.mampu.gov.my.

Heeks, R., 'Information Systems for Public Management: Information Technology and Public Sector Corruption', Working Paper No. 4. Manchester: IDPM—University of Manchester, 1998.

Heeks, R. (ed.), *Reinventing Government in the Information Age: International Practice in IT-Enabled Public Sector*. London: Routledge, 2001.

——, 'Understanding E-Governance for Development', IDPM I-Government Working Paper No. 11, University of Manchester, 2001.

Jongwoo, Han and Kim Hyun Joon, 'Governance of Electronic Governance: The Experi-ences of the United States and Canada', The Maxwell School, Syracuse University, New York.

Kaboolian, L., 'The New Public Management: Challenging the Boundaries of the Management vs Administration Debate', *Public Administration Review*, Vol. 58, No. 3, 1998, pp. 189–93.

Kickert, W.J.M., E. Klign and J.F.M. Koppenjan (eds), *Managing Complex Networks: Strategies for the Public Sector*. London: Sage Publications, 1997.

Kooiman, J., (ed.), *Modern Governance: New Government–Society Interactions*. London: Sage Publications, 1993.

Korac-Kakabadse, Kouzmin A. and A. Korac-Kakabadse, 'Information Technology and Development: Creating "IT Harems", Fostering New Colonialism or solving "wicked" Policy Problems', *Public Administration and Development*, Vol. 20, 2000, pp. 171–84.

Landsbergen Jr., D. and G. Wolken Jr., 'Realizing the Promise: Government Infor-mation Systems and the Fourth Generation of Information Technology', *Public Administration Review*, Vol. 61, No. 2, 2001, pp. 206–20.

Larmour, P. and N. Wolanin (eds), *Corruption & Anti-Corruption*. Canberra: Asia Pacific Press, 2001.

Layne, K. and J. Lee, 'Developing Fully Functional E-Government: A Four Stage Model', *Government Information Quarterly*, Vol. 18, No. ER2, 2001, pp. 122–36.

Lobo, Albert and Suresh Balakrishnan, 'Report Card on Service of Bhoomi Kiosks: An Assessment of Benefits by Users of the Computerized Land Records System in Karnataka', Public Affairs Centre, Bangalore, 2002, http://www1.worldbank.org/publicsector/bnpp/Bhoomi.pdf.

Madon, Shirin and G.R. Kiran, 'Information Technology for Citizen–Government Interface: A Study of Friends Project in Kerala', World Bank, November 2002. http://www1.worldbank.org/publicsector/bnpp/part1.pdf.

McConnell International and WITSA, 'Risk E-Business: Seizing the Opportunity of Global E-Readiness', McConnell International and WITSA, 2000, http://www.mcconnellinternational.com/ereadiness/EReadinessReport.htm.

Miles, Ian and Dieter Kimbel, *Usage Indicators: A New Foundation for Information Technology Policies*. Paris: OECD, 1993.

Silcock, L., 'What is E-Government?', *Parliamentary Affairs*, Vol. 54, No. 1, 2001, pp. 88–101.

Webster, Frank, *Theories of Information Society*. London and New York: Routledge, 1995.

Wescott, C., 'Measuring Governance in Developing Asia', in Lawrence R. Jones, James Guthrie and Peter Steane (eds), *Learning from International Public Management Reform* Vol. 11B, Oxford: JAI–Elsevier Science, 2001, pp. 295–309.

West, D.M., 'Assessing E-Government: The Internet, Democracy, and Service Delivery by State and Federal Governments', Brown University, Providence, 2000, http://www.insidepolitics.org/egovtreport00.html.

World Bank, 'New-Economy Sector Study: Electronic Government and Governance: Lessons for Argentina' World Bank, Washington DC, July 2002, http://www1. worldbank.org/publicsector/egov/Argentina%20Paper%20on%20E-Government.doc.

Annotated List of Web Resources

1. http://www.man.ac.uk/idpm_dp.htm. Richard Heeks, 'Building E-Governance for Development: A Framework for National and Donor Action', I-Government Working Paper Series. This paper discusses the broad issues surrounding information, knowledge, information systems and communication technologies in the process of government.
2. B. Sriram, 'E-Governance: Indian Experiences'. This is a technology paper that traces the growth of e-governance in India. Some cases of e-governance and initiatives of different state governments are discussed.
3. http://www.opt-init.org/partners.html#accenture.
4. http://www.opt-init.org/partners.html#markle.
5. http://www.opt-init.org/partners.html#framework/pages/2.3.3.html.
6. http://www.opt-init.org/partners.html#framework/html.
7. http://www.sdnp.undp.org/it4dev/stories.html.
8. http://www1.worldbank.org/publicsector/egov/. The World Bank's e-government page includes information and case studies from developing countries on e-government organised by country, sector or objectives, as well as links to external studies on e-government many from developed countries.
9. http://www1.oecd.org/puma/pubs/. The OECD's web site offers downloadable reports (in PDF format) on various aspects of government, public participation and ICT including, the OECD Public Management Policy Brief No. 8, 'The Hidden Threat to E-Government: Avoiding Large Government IT Failures' 2001.
10. http://www.egovlinks.com/world_egov_links.html. This portal offers resources on e-government including reports, news and links sorted by category.
11. http://www.man.ac.uk/idpm/idpm_dp.htm#ig. Two online reports that offer a framework and training materials on e-governance for development are available at this link from the University of Manchester.
12. http://www.excelgov.org/techcon/index.htm. The web site for the Inter-Governmental Technology Leadership Consortium of the Council for Excellence in Government has information on e-government, including public surveys from the US and an award competition.
13. http://www.digitalgovernance.org. Digital Governance is a project that explores and disseminates innovative models by which ICT can be used in developing countries to lead to better governance.
14. http://sosig.esrc.bristol.ac.uk/roads/subject-listing/World-cat/polcom.html. This site of the Social Science Information Gateway, part of the UK Resource Discovery Network, offers links to numerous papers, reports, news, governmental and non-governmental organisations addressing e-government.
15. http://www.hicss.hawaii.edu/diglib.htm. The site for the annual Hawaii International Conference on Systems Sciences (HICSS) has a Digital Library with conference papers from all prior HICSS conferences, which includes papers, many technical in nature, on various aspects of ICT, including customer relationship management, e-commerce and ICT for healthcare.

Index

About the Author

Subhash Bhatnagar has been a Professor of Information Systems at the Indian Institute of Management, Ahmedabad (IIMA), for the last 28 years where he has also been CMC Professor in Information Technology, served as the Dean and been a member of the Board of Governors. He was instrumental in establishing and coordinating the activities of two research centres at the IIMA: Centre for Electronic Governance and Telecom Policy Study Centre. At present he divides his time between teaching and research at IIMA and leading an initiative on E-Government at the World Bank.

Professor Bhatnagar's research has focused on ICT for development, e-government and e-commerce. He has published 80 research papers and 7 books. He is the Founder Chairman of the International Federation of Information Processing (IFIP) working group on Social Implications of Computers in Developing Countries and was the Chief Editor of the *International Journal of Information Technology and Development*. He also publishes a quarterly newsletter on *Information Technology in Developing Countries*, is on the editorial boards of half a dozen international journals, and is a recipient of the IFIP Silver Core and the Fellowship of the Computer Society of India.